PRENTICE HALL

AMERICA

PATHWAYS TO THE PRESENT

MODERN AMERICAN HISTORY EDITION

Guided Reading and Review Workbook

Needham, Massachusetts
Upper Saddle River, New Jersey
Glenview, Illinois

ISBN 0-13-067969-0

8 9 10   06 05

GUIDED READING AND REVIEW

Note: Worksheets for Chapters 4–27 correlate directly to the sections in your text. Use worksheets for Chapters 1–3 as appropriate to the content you are teaching/studying.

Success in social studies comes from doing three things well—reading, testing, and writing. The following pages present strategies to help you read for meaning, understand test questions, and write well.

Reading for Meaning

Do you have trouble remembering what you read? Here are some tips from experts that will improve your ability to recall and understand what you read:

BEFORE YOU READ

Preview the text to identify important information.
Like watching the coming attractions at a movie theater, previewing the text helps you know what to expect. Study the questions and strategies below to learn how to preview what you read.

Ask yourself these questions:	Use these strategies to find the answers:
• What is the text about?	Read the headings, subheadings, and captions. Study the photos, maps, tables, or graphs.
• What do I already know about the topic?	Read the questions at the end of the text to see if you can answer any of them.
• What is the purpose of the text?	Turn the headings into *who, what, when, where, why,* or *how* questions. This will help you decide if the text compares things, tells a chain of events, or explains causes and effects.

Organize information in a way that helps you see meaningful connections or relationships.

Taking notes as you read will improve your understanding. Use graphic organizers like the ones below to record the information you read. Study these descriptions and examples to learn how to create each type of organizer.

Sequencing

A **flowchart** helps you see how one event led to another. It can also display the steps in a process.

Use a flowchart if the text—
- tells about a chain of events.
- explains a method of doing something.

TIP▶ List the events or steps in order.

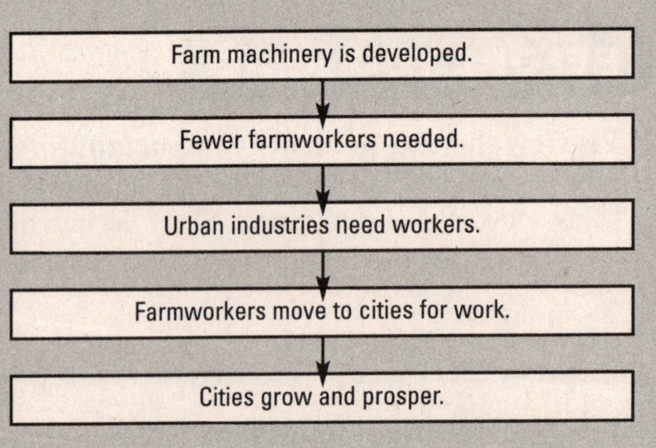

Comparing and Contrasting

A **Venn diagram** displays similarities and differences.

Use a Venn diagram if the text—
- compares and contrasts two individuals, groups, places, things, or events.

TIP▶ Label the outside section of each circle and list differences.
Label the shared section and list similarities.

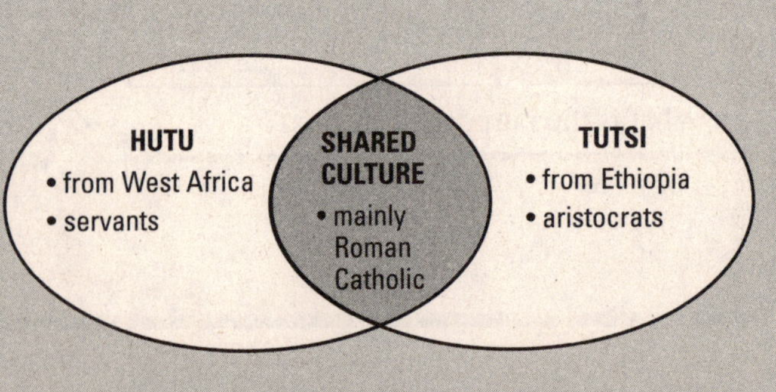

Categorizing Information

A **chart** organizes information in categories.

Use a chart if the text—
- lists similar facts about several places or things.
- presents characteristics of different groups.

TIP▶ Write an appropriate heading for each column in the chart to identify its category.

COUNTRY	FORM OF GOVERNMENT	ECONOMY
Cuba	communist dictatorship	command economy
Puerto Rico	democracy	free enterprise system

Identifying Main Ideas and Details

A **concept web** helps you understand relationships among ideas.

Use a concept web if the text—
- provides examples to support a main idea.
- links several ideas to a main topic.

TIP▶ Write the main idea in the largest circle. Write details in smaller circles and draw lines to show relationships.

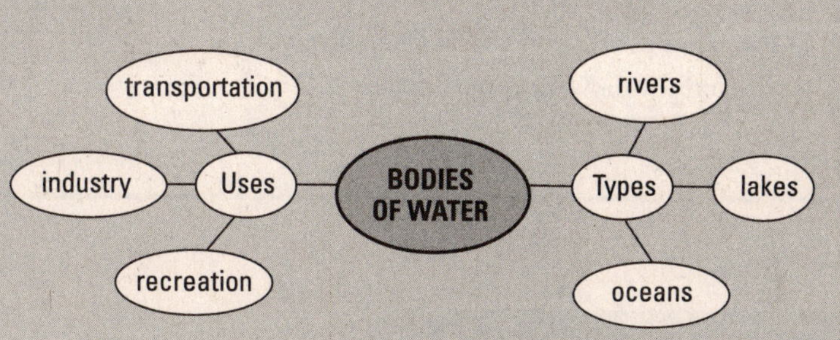

Organizing Information

An **outline** provides an overview, or a kind of blueprint for reading.

Use an outline to organize ideas—
- according to their importance.
- according to the order in which they are presented.

TIP▶ Use Roman numerals for main ideas, capital letters for secondary ideas, and Arabic numerals for supporting details.

> **I. Differences Between the North and the South**
>   **A.** Views on slavery
>   **1.** Northern abolitionists
>   **2.** Southern slave owners
>   **B.** Economies
>   **1.** Northern manufacturing
>   **2.** Southern agriculture

Identifying Cause and Effect

A **cause-and-effect** diagram shows the relationship between what happened (effect) and the reason why it happened (cause).

Use a cause-and-effect chart if the text—
- lists one or more causes for an event.
- lists one or more results of an event.

TIP▶ Label causes and effects. Draw arrows to indicate how ideas are related.

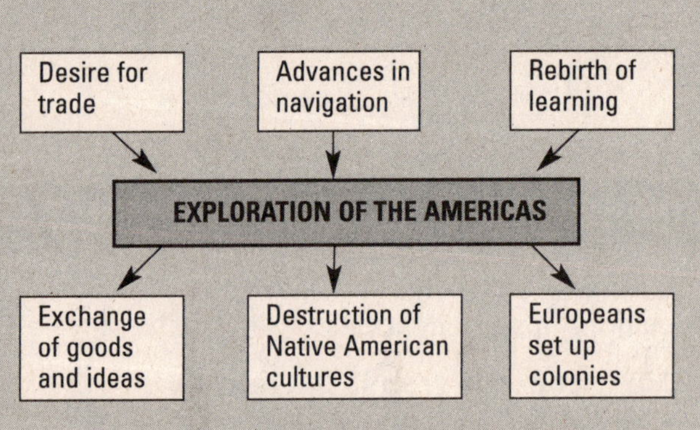

AFTER YOU READ

Test yourself to find out what you learned from reading the text.
Go back to the questions you asked yourself before you read the text. You should be able to give more complete answers to these questions:
- What is the text about?
- What is the purpose of the text?

You should also be able to make connections between the new information you learned from the text and what you already knew about the topic.

Study your graphic organizer. Use this information as the *answers*. Make up a meaningful *question* about each piece of information.

Taking Tests

*Do you panic at the thought of taking a standardized test?
Here are some tips that most test developers recommend to
help you achieve good scores.*

MULTIPLE-CHOICE QUESTIONS

**Read each part of a multiple-choice question to make sure you
understand what is being asked.**

Many tests are made up of multiple-choice questions. Some multiple-choice
items are **direct questions.** They are complete sentences followed by possible
answers, called distractors.

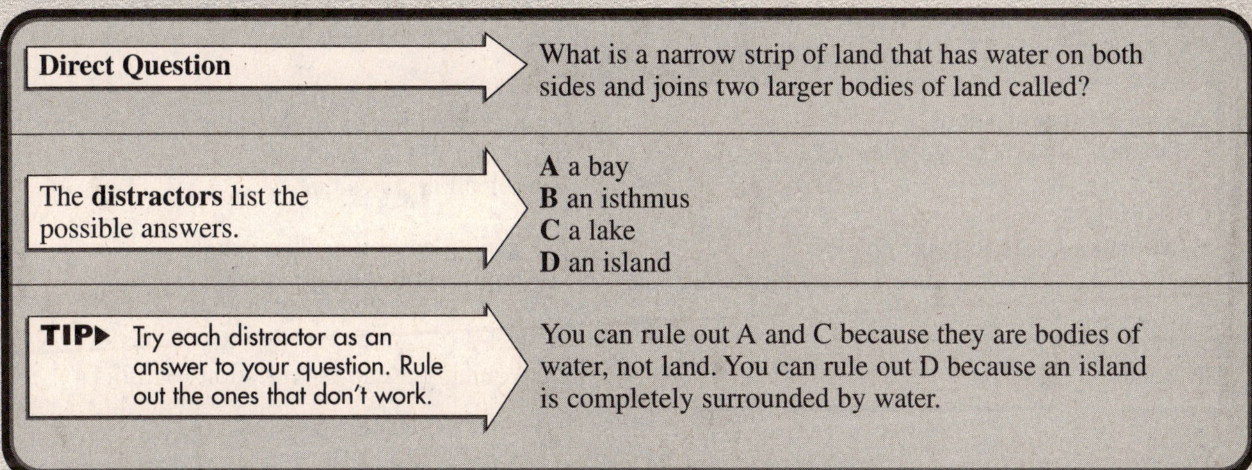

Other multiple-choice questions are **incomplete sentences** that you are to
finish. They are followed by possible answers.

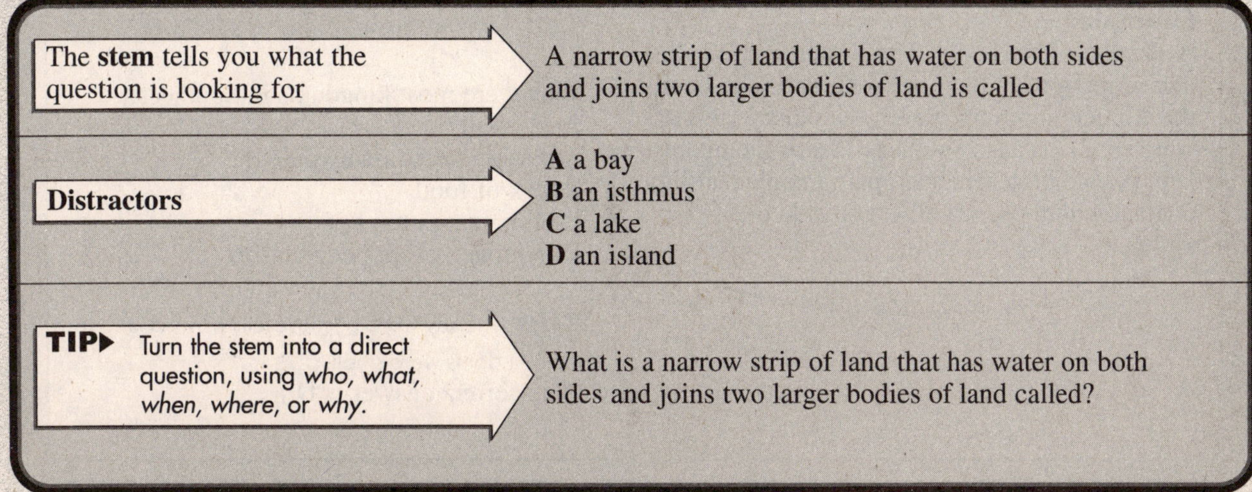

Identify the type of question you are being asked.

Social studies tests often ask questions that involve reading comprehension.
Other questions may require you to gather or interpret information from a
map, graph, or chart. The following strategies will help you answer different
kinds of questions.

Reading Comprehension Questions

What to do:

1. Determine the content and organization of the selection.

How to do it:

Read the **title.** Skim the selection. Look for key words that indicate time, cause-and-effect, or comparison.

2. Analyze the questions. Do they ask you to *recall facts?*

Look for **key words** in the stem:
<u>According to</u> the selection . . .
The selection <u>states</u> that . . .

Do they ask you to *make judgments?*

The <u>main idea</u> of the selection is . . .
The author <u>would likely</u> agree that . . .

3. Read the selection.

Read quickly. Keep the questions in mind.

4. Answer the questions.

Try out each distractor and choose the best answer. Refer back to the selection if necessary.

Example:

A Region of Diversity The Khmer empire was one of many kingdoms in Southeast Asia. Unlike the Khmer empire, however, the other kingdoms were small because Southeast Asia's mountains kept people protected and apart. People had little contact with those who lived outside their own valley.

Why were most kingdoms in Southeast Asia small?
A disease killed many people
B lack of food
C climate was too hot
D mountains kept people apart

TIP▶ The key word <u>because</u> tells why the kingdoms were small.
(The correct answer is D.)

Map Questions

What to do: | **How to do it:**

1. Determine what kind of information is presented on the map.

Read the map **title.** It will indicate the purpose of the map.
Study the **map key.** It will explain the symbols used on the map.
Look at the **scale.** It will help you calculate distance between places on the map.

2. Read the question. Determine which component on the map will help you find the answer.

Look for **key words** in the stem.
About <u>how far</u> . . . [use the scale]
<u>What crops</u> were grown in . . . [use the map key]

3. Look at the map and answer the question in your own words.

Do not read the distractors yet.

4. Choose the best answer.

Decide which distractor agrees with the answer you determined from the map.

Eastern Europe: Language Groups

In which of these countries are Thraco-Illyrian languages spoken?

A Romania
B Albania
C Hungary
D Lithuania

TIP▶ Read the labels and the key to understand the map.
(The correct answer is B.)

What to do:

1. Determine the purpose of the graph.

How to do it:
Read the graph **title.** It indicates what the graph represents.

2. Determine what information on the graph will help you find the answer.

Read the **labels** on the graph or on the key. They tell the units of measurement used by the graph.

3. Choose the best answer.

Decide which distractor agrees with the answer you determined from the graph.

Example

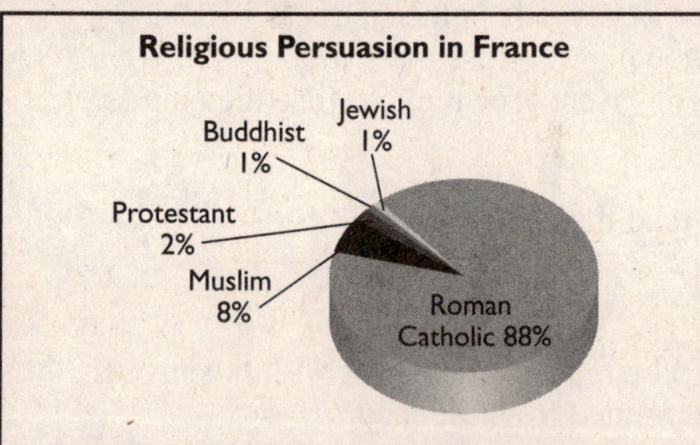

A **Circle graph** shows the relationship of parts to the whole in terms of percentages.

After Roman Catholics, the next largest religious population in France is
A Buddhist   C Jewish
B Protestant   D Muslim

TIP▶ Compare the percentages listed in the labels.
(The correct answer is D.)

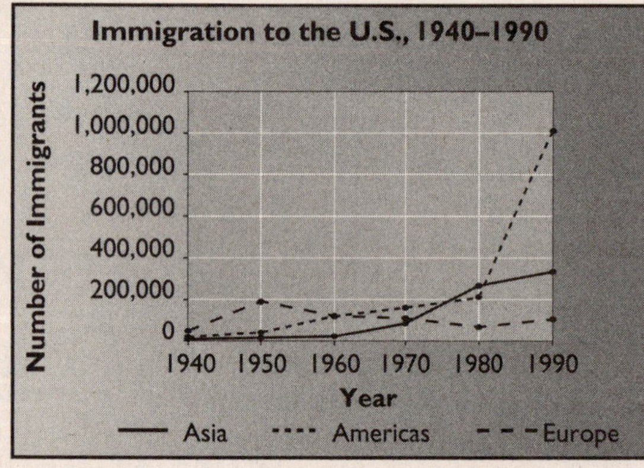

A **line graph** shows a pattern or change over time by the direction of the line.

Between 1980 and 1990, immigration to the U.S. from the Americas
A decreased a little   C stayed about the same
B increased greatly   D increased a little

TIP▶ Compare the vertical distance between the two correct points on the line graph.
(The correct answer is B.)

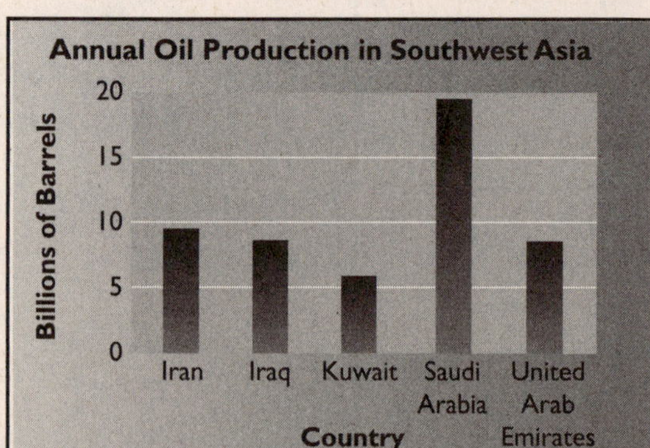

A **bar graph** compares differences in quantity by showing bars of different lengths.

Saudi Arabia produces about how many more billion of barrels of oil a year than Iran?
A 5 million   C 15 million
B 10 million   D 20 million

TIP▶ Compare the heights of the bars to find the difference.
(The correct answer is B.)

Writing for Social Studies

When you face a writing assignment, do you think, "How will I ever get through this?" Here are some tips to guide you through any writing project from start to finish.

THE WRITING PROCESS

Follow each step of the writing process to communicate effectively.

Step 1. Prewrite

- Establish the purpose.
- Define the topic.
- Determine the audience.
- Gather details.

Step 2. Draft

- Organize information logically in an outline or graphic organizer.
- Write an introduction, body, and conclusion.
- State main ideas clearly.
- Include relevant details to support your ideas.

Step 3. Revise

- Edit for clarity of ideas and elaboration.

Step 4. Proofread

- Correct any errors in spelling, grammar, and punctuation.

Step 5. Publish and Present

- Copy text neatly by hand, or use a typewriter or word processor.
- Illustrate as needed.
- Create a cover, if appropriate.

TYPES OF WRITING FOR SOCIAL STUDIES

Identify the purpose for your writing.

Each type of writing assignment has a specific purpose, and each purpose needs a different plan for development. The following descriptions and examples will help you identify the three purposes for social studies writing. The lists of steps will help you plan your writing.

Writing to Inform

Purpose: to present facts or ideas

Example

During the 1960s, research indicated the dangers of the insecticide DDT. It killed insects but also had long-term effects. When birds and fish ate poisoned insects, DDT built up in their fatty tissue. The poison also showed up in human beings who ate birds and fish contaminated by DDT.

TIP▶ Look for these **key terms** in the assignment: explain, describe, report, narrate

How to get started:
- Determine the topic you will write about.
- Write a topic sentence that tells the main idea.
- List all the ideas you can think of that are related to the topic.
- Arrange the ideas in logical order.

Writing to Persuade

Purpose: to influence someone

Example

Teaching computer skills in the classroom uses time that could be spent teaching students how to think for themselves or how to interact with others. Students who can reason well, express themselves clearly, and get along with other people will be better prepared for life than those who can use a computer.

TIP▶ Look for these **key terms** in the assignment: convince, argue, request

How to get started:
- Make sure you understand the problem or issue clearly.
- Determine your position.
- List evidence to support your arguments.
- Predict opposing views.
- List evidence you can use to overcome the opposing arguments.

Writing to Provide Historical Interpretations

Purpose: to present the perspective of someone in a different era

Example

The crossing took a week, but the steamship voyage was hard. We were cramped in steerage with hundreds of others. At last we saw the huge statue of the lady with the torch. In the reception center, my mother held my hand while the doctor examined me. Then, my father showed our papers to the official, and we collected our bags. I was scared as we headed off to find a home in our new country.

TIP▶ Look for these **key terms** in the assignment: go back in time, create, suppose that, if you were

How to get started:
- Study the events or issues of the time period you will write about.
- Consider how these events or issues might have affected different people at the time.
- Choose a person whose views you would like to present.
- Identify the thoughts and feelings this person might have experienced.

RESEARCH FOR WRITING

Follow each step of the writing process to communicate effectively.

After you have identified the purpose for your writing, you may need to do research. The following steps will help you plan, gather, organize, and present information.

Step 1. Ask Questions

Ask yourself questions to help guide your research.	What do I already know about the topic? What do I want to find out about the topic?

Step 2. Acquire Information

Locate and use appropriate sources of information about the topic.	Library Internet search Interviews
Take notes.	Follow accepted format for listing sources.

Step 3. Analyze Information

Evaluate the information you find.	Is it relevant to the topic? Is it up-to-date? Is it accurate? Is the writer an authority on the topic? Is there any bias?

Step 4. Use Information

Answer your research questions with the information you have found. (You may find that you need to do more research.)	Do I have all the information I need?
Organize your information into the main points you want to make. Identify supporting details.	Arrange ideas in outline form or in a graphic organizer.

Step 5. Communicate What You've Learned

Review the purpose for your writing and choose an appropriate way to present the information.	**Purpose**	**Presentation**
	inform	formal paper, documentary, multimedia
	persuade	essay, letter to the editor, speech
	interpret	journal, newspaper account, drama
Draft and revise your writing, and then evaluate it.	Use a rubric for self-evaluation.	

EVALUATING YOUR WRITING

Use the following rubric to help you evaluate your writing.

	Excellent	Good	Acceptable	Unacceptable
Purpose	Achieves purpose—to inform, persuade, or provide historical interpretation—very well	Informs, persuades, or provides historical interpretation reasonably well	Reader cannot easily tell if the purpose is to inform, persuade, or provide historical interpretation	Lacks purpose
Organization	Develops ideas in a very clear and logical way	Presents ideas in a reasonably well-organized way	Reader has difficulty following the organization	Lacks organization
Elaboration	Explains all ideas with facts and details	Explains most ideas with facts and details	Includes some supporting facts and details	Lacks supporting details
Use of Language	Uses excellent vocabulary and sentence structure with no errors in spelling, grammar, or punctuation	Uses good vocabulary and sentence structure with very few errors in spelling, grammar, or punctuation	Includes some errors in grammar, punctuation, and spelling	Includes many errors in grammar, punctuation, and spelling

The Native American World

A. AS YOU READ

Complete the chart below as you read Section 1. For each region listed, briefly describe the local environment and the culture(s) that developed there.

REGION	ENVIRONMENT	CULTURE(S)
1. The North		
2. The Northwest Coast		
3. California		
4. The Plateau		
5. The Great Basin		
6. The Southwest		
7. The Plains		
8. The Northeast		
9. The Southeast		

B. REVIEWING KEY TERMS

Explain how each term relates to Native American culture.

10. migration ____

11. kinship ____

12. clan ____

13. oral history ____

14. barter ____

GUIDED READING AND REVIEW

The European World

A. AS YOU READ

Fill in the boxes below to organize information about European society in the 1400s. Under each main idea, write two supporting ideas from Section 2.

Main Idea A: Feudalism and the Roman Catholic Church were the most important institutions during the Early Middle Ages.

Main Idea B: The growth of Europe's economy in the Late Middle Ages produced huge changes.

Main Idea C: The Renaissance was a time of great learning and artistic accomplishment.

B. REVIEWING KEY TERMS

Complete each sentence by writing the correct term or name in the blank provided.

1. In the European system called _______________, lords protected the serfs who farmed their land.

2. The rebirth of a spirit of creativity, exploration, and learning marked the period known as the _______________.

3. The Church organized the _______________ to gain control of the holy city of Jerusalem from the Turks.

4. The power of the_______________, or rulers who reign over states or territories, was increased by Europe's growing wealth in the Late Middle Ages.

The World of the West Africans

A. AS YOU READ
As you read Section 3, answer the following questions on the lines provided.

1. What items did West Africans and Europeans trade? __________________________

____

2. What three types of climate regions influenced life in West Africa? ____________

____

3. What religious beliefs did traditional African cultures have in common? ________

____

4. Describe the government of Benin. ____

____

5. Describe the government of Songhai. ____

____

6. How were European and African attitudes toward land and people different? ______

____

7. Describe how the African concept of slavery differed from slavery in the Americas. ______

____

____

B. REVIEWING KEY TERMS
Briefly define each of the following.

8. savanna ____

9. lineage ____

10. scarce ____

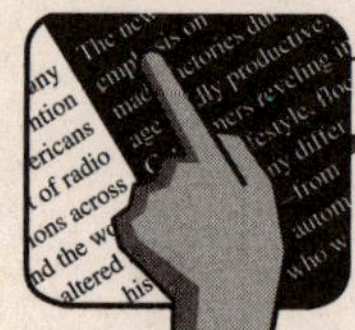

The Atlantic World Is Born

A. As You Read

Below are four main ideas from Section 4. As you read, fill in two supporting details under each main idea.

Main Idea: Spanish clergy and nobles had strong reasons for wanting Columbus to succeed in his voyage.

1. ____

2. ____

Main Idea: Columbus achieved far more success as an admiral than as a governor.

3. ____

4. ____

Main Idea: The impact of Columbus's voyages was both good and bad.

5. ____

6. ____

Main Idea: The need for laborers in the Western Hemisphere led to the enslavement of millions of West Africans.

7. ____

8. ____

B. Reviewing Key Terms

Explain how each of the following relates to the interaction among Europeans, Native Americans, and West Africans after 1492.

9. Columbian Exchange ____

10. Treaty of Tordesillas ____

11. plantation ____

12. cash crop ____

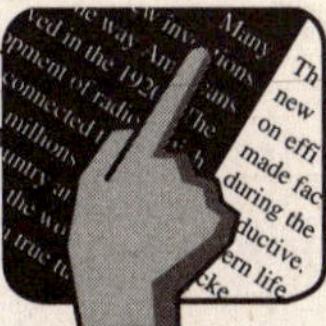

Spanish Explorers and Colonies

A. As You Read

As you read Section 1, complete the chart below by filling in information about Spanish exploration of the Americas between 1492 and 1650.

Explorers/Settlers	Area of Exploration, Conquest, and/or Settlement	Reason for Exploration or Settlement
1. Ponce de Léon		
2. Balboa		
3. Magellan		
4. Cortés		
5. Pizarro		
6. Cabeza de Vaca and Estevanico		
7. Coronado		
8. De Soto		
9. Menendéz de Avilés		
10. Juan de Oñate		
11. missionaries and soldiers		

B. Reviewing Key Terms

Explain how each of the following relates to the Spanish conquest of the Americas.

12. colony ____

13. isthmus ____

14. hidalgo ____

15. conquistador ____

16. mestizo ____

17. presidio ____

18. mission ____

19. Pueblo Revolt of 1680 ____

GUIDED READING AND REVIEW

Jamestown

A. As You Read

As you read Section 2, fill in the missing information about English exploration
and the early Virginia colony.

EXPLORATION AND EARLY SETTLEMENTS
1. Reasons for English exploration:
2. Why the Roanoke Island Colony was a disaster:

THE JAMESTOWN SETTLEMENT STRUGGLES
3. Conflict with Native Americans:
4. Unrealistic expectations:
5. The failure of the Virginia Company:

GROWING TOBACCO
6. Role in Virginia's economy:
7. Labor force:

BACON'S REBELLION
8. Causes:

B. Reviewing Key Terms

Briefly identify each of the following.

9. privateer ____

10. charter ____

11. joint-stock company _______________________________________

12. royal colony ____

13. legislature ____

14. House of Burgesses _______________________________________

15. indentured servant _______________________________________

16. Bacon's Rebellion ____

The New England Colonies

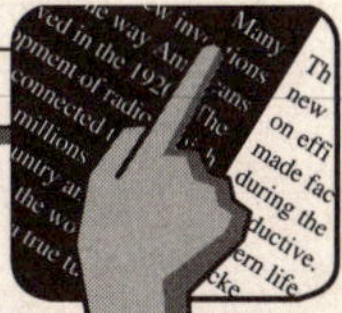

A. As You Read

Below are three main ideas from Section 3. As you read, fill in two supporting details under each main idea.

Main Idea: The fur trade had a significant impact on both the French and the Native Americans.

1. ____

2. ____

Main Idea: The Puritans had definite ideas about religion and about the kind of society they wanted to establish.

3. ____

4. ____

Main Idea: Native Americans tried to resist the English settlers, who were forcing them out of their homelands.

5. ____

6. ____

B. Reviewing Key Terms

Use each of the following in a sentence that shows how the term or name relates to the early colonization of North America.

7. persecute ____

8. Pilgrim ____

9. Mayflower Compact ____

10. Great Migration ____

11. religious tolerance ______________________________________

12. Salem witch trials _______________________________________

13. Pequot War ____

14. King Philip's War ____

The Middle and Southern Colonies

A. AS YOU READ

Complete the chart below as you read Section 4. For each colony describe why it
was settled and where the settlers came from.

Colony	Reason for Settlement	Origin of Settlers
1. New Netherland/New York		
2. Pennsylvania		
3. Delaware		
4. Maryland		
5. The Carolinas		
6. Georgia		

B. REVIEWING KEY TERMS

Define or identify each of the following.

7. Middle Colonies ____

8. diversity ____

9. synagogue ____

10. proprietary colony ____

11. Quaker ____

12. haven ____

13. Southern Colonies ____

14. trustee ____

An Empire and Its Colonies

A. AS YOU READ

As you read Section 1, answer the following questions on the lines provided.

1. Why did mercantilists consider colonies so important?

____

2. How did England tighten control over colonial trade?

____

3. What effect did mercantilism have on European politics?

____

4. Why were the governors of England's royal colonies not really the dominant power holders?

____

5. How did geography affect the economies of Britain's colonies in America?

____

6. Why did the Southern Colonies become increasingly dependent on enslaved Africans?

____

B. REVIEWING KEY TERMS

Briefly define the following terms.

7. mercantilism ____

8. balance of trade ____

9. duty ____

10. salutary neglect ____

11. staple crop ____

12. triangular trade ____

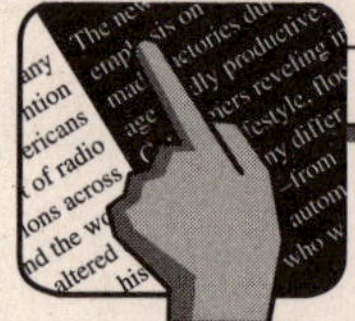

GUIDED READING AND REVIEW

Life in Colonial America

A. As You Read

As you read Section 2, write two supporting details under each of the following main ideas.

One concept that American colonists brought from Europe was the belief that people are not equal.

1. ____

2. ____

While some people in the colonies developed specialized skills and trades, others lived off the land and sea.

3. ____

4. ____

Women in colonial society had few rights.

5. ____

6. ____

Women played an important role in the household and the community.

7. ____

8. ____

Hard work was required to survive in the colonies.

9. ____

10. ____

The colonial education system was very different from our modern-day school system.

11. ____

12. ____

B. Reviewing Key Terms

Identify each of the following terms.

13. gentry ____

14. apprentice ____

15. almanac ____

16. indigo ____

17. self-sufficient ____

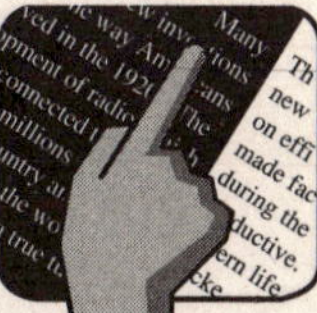

African Americans in the Colonies

A. As You Read

As you read Section 3, fill in the missing information below about African Americans in the colonies.

In South Carolina and Georgia
1. Work performed:
2. Proportion of population:
3. Culture:
4. Family relationships:

In Virginia and Maryland
5. Work performed:
6. Proportion of population:
7. Culture:
8. Family relationships:

In The New England And Middle Colonies
9. Work performed:
10. Proportion of population:

B. Reviewing Key Terms

Use each term below in a sentence that shows the meaning of the term.

11. Middle Passage ____

12. Stono Rebellion ____

GUIDED READING AND REVIEW

Emerging Tensions

A. As You Read

As you read Section 4, fill in three facts relating to each main idea.

Main Idea: By the mid-1700s, English colonists began to move inland from the Atlantic Coast.

1. ____

2. ____

3. ____

Main Idea: Tension increased among Native Americans, the French, and the British as British settlers migrated westward.

4. ____

5. ____

6. ____

Main Idea: The mid-1700s brought significant changes to religious life in the colonies.

7. ____

8. ____

9. ____

B. Reviewing Key Terms

Explain how each of the following is related to life in early eighteenth-century colonial America.

10. immigrant ____

11. Great Awakening ____

12. itinerant ____

13. dissent ____

The French and Indian War

A. AS YOU READ

As you read Section 1, fill in two supporting facts under each main idea.

Rivalry between Britain and France led to the French and Indian War.

1. ____

2. ____

By about 1758 the tide of war began to turn in British favor.

3. ____

4. ____

Despite victory, the war strained relations between the British and the American colonists.

5. ____

6. ____

B. REVIEWING KEY TERMS

Identify or define each of the following terms.

7. French and Indian War _______________________________________

8. Albany Plan of Union _______________________________________

9. militia _______________________________________

10. prime minister _______________________________________

11. siege _______________________________________

12. Treaty of Paris (1763) _______________________________________

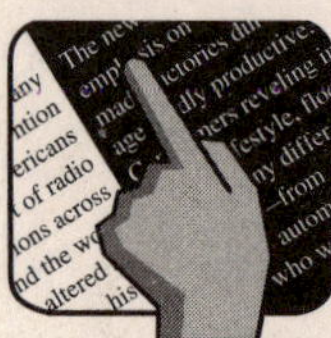

Issues Behind the Revolution

A. As You Read

Write in the missing cause or effect as you read Section 2.

1. Cause: The British military commander, General Jeffrey Amherst, stopped the flow of trade goods to Native Americans.	**1. Effect:** _________________________
2. Cause: _________________________	**2. Effect:** In 1764 Parliament passed the Sugar Act to raise more tax money for Britain.
3. Cause: _________________________	**3. Effect:** Colonists boycotted British goods and claimed they could not be taxed without being represented in Parliament.
4. Cause: After Britain sent troops to Boston to stop resistance to the Townsend Acts, tensions exploded in the Boston Massacre of 1770.	**4. Effect:** _________________________
5. Cause: Parliament passed the Tea Act.	**5. Effect:** _________________________
6. Cause: _________________________	**6. Effect:** Protest committees sent delegates to the First Continental Congress.

B. Reviewing Key Terms

Explain how each of the following contributed to the deteriorating relationship between Britain and its American colonies.

7. Pontiac's Rebellion ____

8. Proclamation of 1763 ____

9. Boston Massacre ____

10. Battles of Lexington and Concord ____

Ideas Behind the Revolution

A. AS YOU READ

As you read Section 3, draw a line through the term or name in each group that is not related to the others. Explain how the remaining terms or names are related.

1. independence   Olive Branch Petition   *Common Sense*   Thomas Paine

____

____

2. John Dickinson   John Locke   Thomas Jefferson   Declaration of Independence

____

____

3. natural rights   social contract theory   Enlightenment   John Locke

____

____

4. Abigail Adams   preamble   John Adams   women's rights

____

____

B. REVIEWING KEY TERMS

Briefly identify or define the following key terms.

5. *Common Sense* ____

6. Second Continental Congress _______________________________________

7. Olive Branch Petition _______________________________________

8. Declaration of Independence _______________________________________

9. Enlightenment _______________________________________

10. natural rights _______________________________________

GUIDED READING AND REVIEW

Fighting for Independence

A. AS YOU READ

As you read Section 4, fill in the missing information about the War for
Independence.

STRENGTHS AND WEAKNESSES
1. British:
2. Americans:

BATTLE OUTCOMES AND SIGNIFICANCE
3. Bunker Hill:
4. Trenton:
5. Saratoga:

B. REVIEWING KEY TERMS

Briefly identify or describe each of the following.

6. Battle of Bunker Hill ____

7. casualty ____

8. Loyalist ____

9. mercenary ____

10. Battle of Trenton ____

11. Battle of Saratoga ____

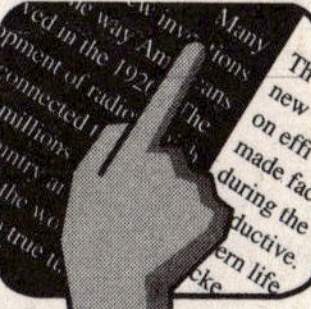

Winning Independence

A. AS YOU READ

As you read Section 5, answer the following questions on the lines provided.

1. What hardships did Americans face during the war?

____

2. Why was the fighting that took place in the South particularly vicious?

____

3. How did the Americans defeat Cornwallis in the Battle of Yorktown?

____

4. What were the major provisions of the Treaty of Paris?

____

5. What impact did the Revolution have on African Americans?

____

6. How did the outcome of the Revolution affect Native Americans?

____

B. REVIEWING KEY TERMS

Briefly explain how each of the following is related to the War for Independence.

7. blockade _______________________________________

8. profiteering _____________________________________

9. inflation _______________________________________

10. Battle of Yorktown _______________________________

11. Treaty of Paris (1783) _____________________________

Government by the States

A. AS YOU READ

As you read Section 1, fill in two supporting facts under each main idea statement.

> **Main Idea:** Once the Revolution was over, few Americans wanted, or saw the
> need for, a strong national government.

1. ____

2. ____

> **Main Idea:** Some Americans expressed concerns about weaknesses in the
> Articles of Confederation.

3. ____

4. ____

> **Main Idea:** Shays' Rebellion convinced many Americans that a stronger
> national government was necessary.

5. ____

6. ____

B. REVIEWING KEY TERMS

Use each of the following terms in a sentence that explains its meaning.

7. Articles of Confederation _______________________________________

8. legislative branch ____

9. executive branch ____

10. judicial branch ____

11. constitution ____

12. republic ____

13. Shays' Rebellion ____

14. specie ____

The Constitutional Convention

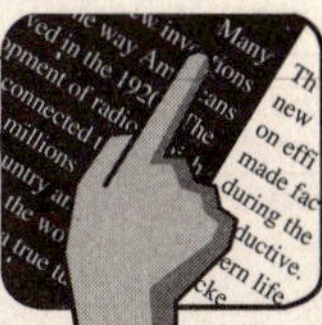

A. As You Read

As you read Section 2, check the sentence in each group that is not related to the other sentences. Then write another related sentence on the line provided.

GROUP 1

_____ **a.** James Madison saw people as naturally selfish and driven by powerful emotions.

_____ **b.** James Madison believed proper government would bring order to society.

_____ **c.** James Madison was happily married for 42 years.

_____ **d.** James Madison supported a strong national government.

____

GROUP 2

_____ **a.** The Three-Fifths Compromise solved the problem of southern representation in the House of Representatives.

_____ **b.** Delegates chose George Washington to be convention president.

_____ **c.** Divisions among the convention delegates were resolved by compromise.

_____ **d.** The Great Compromise created the House of Representatives and the Senate.

____

GROUP 3

_____ **a.** By running for election every six years, senators were less likely to follow the whims of popular opinion.

_____ **b.** Members of the House of Representatives were kept responsive to the wishes of the people by having to run for reelection every two years.

_____ **c.** The election of President was removed from direct control of the people.

_____ **d.** The elastic clause gives Congress wide-ranging power to make laws.

____

B. Reviewing Key Terms

Explain each of the following terms on a separate sheet of paper.

4. amend   **5.** veto   **6.** Great Compromise   **7.** Three-Fifths Compromise   **8.** federal system of government   **9.** separation of powers   **10.** checks and balances   **11.** Electoral College

Ratifying the Constitution

A. As You Read

As you read Section 3, answer the following questions on the lines provided.

1. Why did the Framers of the Constitution want ratification votes cast by special state conventions rather than by state legislatures?

____

2. What response did James Madison and Alexander Hamilton have for people who feared the federal government's power over the states?

____

3. Why did the anti-Federalists oppose the Constitution?

____

4. What factors helped the Federalists win approval for the Constitution?

____

5. Why did Federalists object to the Bill of Rights?

____

6. Why did the anti-Federalists support the Bill of Rights?

____

B. Reviewing Key Terms

Define each of the following.

7. ratify ____

8. Federalist ____

9. faction ____

10. anti-Federalist ____

11. Bill of Rights ____

The New Government

A. As You Read

Each of the following sentences contains one or more errors. As you read Section 4, rewrite each sentence to make it correct.

1. President Washington chose Thomas Jefferson to be Attorney General and Alexander Hamilton to head the Department of State.

____

2. Thomas Jefferson was a strict Federalist whose main concern was the central government rather than individuals' rights.

____

3. Despite the adoption of the Constitution, the new nation remained unstable.

____

4. Washington soon lost popularity and was not reelected.

____

5. During its early years, the nation's capital was established in Boston.

____

6. Thomas Jefferson appointed Pierre-Charles L'Enfant to the commission formed to survey the city that became the nation's capital.

____

B. Reviewing Key Terms

Identify each of the following.

7. inauguration ____

8. Cabinet ____

9. domestic affairs ____

10. administration ____

11. precedent ____

Liberty Versus Order in the 1790s

A. AS YOU READ

As you read Section 1, answer the following questions on the lines provided.

1. What was Hamilton's plan for paying off the Revolutionary War debt?

____

2. Why did some Americans oppose Hamilton's plan?

____

3. How did the French Revolution divide Americans?

____

4. Why was Jay's Treaty controversial?

____

5. Why did the Whiskey Rebellion occur?

____

6. Who were the Jeffersonian Republicans?

____

B. REVIEWING KEY TERMS

Define each of the following terms.

7. tariff ____

8. interest ____

9. strict construction ____

10. loose construction ____

11. neutral ____

12. Jay's Treaty ____

13. Whiskey Rebellion ____

14. political party____

The Election of 1800

A. AS YOU READ

As you read Section 2, check the sentence in each group that is not related to the other sentences. Then write another related sentence on the line provided.

GROUP 1

_____ **a.** During the crisis atmosphere of war, the Federalists passed a number of acts that strengthened the federal government.

_____ **b.** The Federalists increased the size of the armed forces and raised taxes.

_____ **c.** Asking for a bribe was common practice in European diplomacy.

_____ **d.** The Federalists passed the Alien and Sedition Acts of 1798.

____

GROUP 2

_____ **a.** Gabriel Prosser, with other enslaved people, planned a revolt in Richmond, Virginia.

_____ **b.** John Adams attempted to reduce hostilities with France.

_____ **c.** The rebellion failed and the leader, along with other rebels, was executed.

_____ **d.** African Americans embraced the discussion of liberty all around them.

____

GROUP 3

_____ **a.** The election of 1800 was decided in the House of Representatives.

_____ **b.** The real winner of the election of 1800 was the Constitution.

_____ **c.** With the election of 1800, the Jeffersonian Republicans gained control of the Congress and the presidency.

_____ **d.** In 1801 the new capital was a swamp with half-completed buildings.

____

B. REVIEWING KEY TERMS

Identify each of the following.

4. XYZ affair ____

5. Alien and Sedition Acts _______________________________________

6. Virginia and Kentucky Resolutions ______________________________

7. nullification ____

The Jefferson Administration

A. AS YOU READ

Below are four main ideas from Section 3. As you read, fill in two supporting facts under each main idea.

> **Main Idea:** Jefferson's main goal when he took office was to reduce the power of the federal government.

1. ____

2. ____

> **Main Idea:** In *Marbury* v. *Madison*, Chief Justice John Marshall set a number of important precedents in constitutional law.

3. ____

4. ____

> **Main Idea:** Jefferson used the power of the federal government to encourage westward expansion.

5. ____

6. ____

> **Main Idea:** Jefferson's trade embargo was widely disliked by Americans.

7. ____

8. ____

B. REVIEWING KEY TERMS

Explain the significance of each of the following terms in Jefferson's presidency or in the expansion of the United States.

9. agenda ____

10. bureaucracy ____

11. *Marbury* v. *Madison* ____

12. judicial review ____

13. Louisiana Purchase ____

14. Lewis and Clark expedition ______________________________________

15. embargo ____

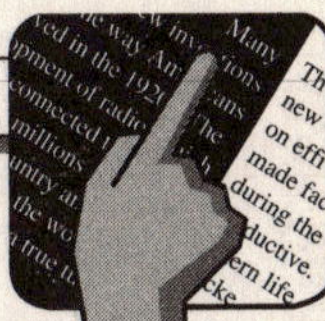

Native American Resistance

A. AS YOU READ

As you read Section 4, mark each statement in the table below either true or false.
If a statement is false, correct the statement.

Statement	True or False	Correct Statement
1. In 1794 the victory of Native Americans at the Battle of Fallen Timbers strengthened their resistance to American expansion.		
2. Little Turtle, a leader of the Miami people, adopted some of the Americans' customs and tried to live peacefully with the settlers.		
3. Handsome Lake called on the Seneca to give up their culture and adopt white American ideas about land, agriculture, and family.		
4. Tenskwatawa rejected Native American ways and established a settlement in Canada.		
5. Tecumseh believed that the Native Americans' only hope of resisting American expansion was to unite.		

B. REVIEWING KEY TERMS

Define or identify each of the following.

6. Treaty of Greenville ____

7. reservation ____

8. assimilation ____

9. Battle of Tippecanoe ____

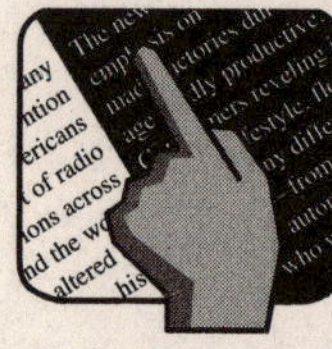

GUIDED READING AND REVIEW

The War of 1812

A. AS YOU READ

As you read Section 5, write one or two sentences to support each of the following main ideas.

1. Anger toward the British led President Madison to call for war. ________________________

____

____

2. Despite some success in the naval war, the Americans soon had to acknowledge the superiority of the British navy. ____

____

____

3. Critics of "Mr. Madison's War" pointed out how much damage it had done to the nation.

____

4. The Battle of New Orleans had a positive outcome for the United States. ____________

____

____

5. The United States experienced its first depression in 1819. _______________________

____

____

6. The debate concerning the admission of the state of Missouri to the United States was settled through compromise. ____

____

B. REVIEWING KEY TERMS

Identify each of the following.

7. impressment ____

8. War of 1812 ____

9. Treaty of Ghent ____

10. Battle of New Orleans ____

11. depression ____

12. Missouri Compromise ____

Cultural, Social, and Religious Life

A. As You Read

As you read Section 1, answer the following questions on the lines provided.

1. How did Noah Webster contribute to the advancement of education?

____

____

2. What virtues did the American people think were needed in the new republic?

____

____

3. To what extent had American attitudes toward the role of women in society changed from colonial times to the early 1800s?

____

____

4. What kinds of social changes did the republic experience in its early days?

____

____

5. Why did many women become actively involved in the religious movement of the 1800s?

____

____

6. What effect did African Americans joining Christian churches have on religious services?

____

____

B. Reviewing Key Terms

Briefly define each of the following terms.

7. mobile society ____

8. Second Great Awakening ____

9. evangelical ____

10. congregation ____

11. revival ____

12. denomination ____

GUIDED READING AND REVIEW

Trails to the West

A. AS YOU READ

All of the following sentences are incorrect. As you read Section 2, rewrite each sentence to make it correct.

1. The movement of American settlers to land west of the Appalachians had little impact on Native Americans.

____

2. Events in South America had no bearing on Spain's decision to give up Florida to the United States.

____

3. Until about 1850, only the United States expressed interest in the Oregon Country.

____

4. The main reason that people headed west along the Oregon Trail was that the frontier offered a pleasant climate.

____

5. The Mormons eventually prospered as miners in California.

____

6. The gold rush was a disaster for cities along the Pacific Coast.

____

B. REVIEWING KEY TERMS

Briefly define or identify each of the following.

7. cede ____

8. manifest destiny____

9. mountain man ____

10. Oregon Trail ____

11. pass ____

12. California Gold Rush ____________________________________

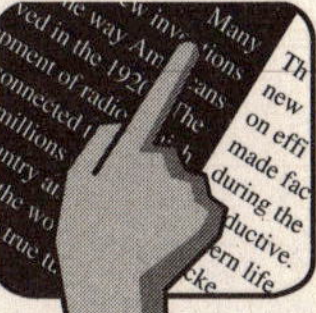

The Great Plains and the Southwest

A. As You Read

Below are four main ideas from Section 3. As you read, fill in two supporting details under each main idea.

Main Idea: The arrival of Europeans changed the lives of the Native Americans who lived on the Great Plains.

1. ____

2. ____

Main Idea: The Spanish tried to gain control of the area that is now California.

3. ____

4. ____

Main Idea: Though Spain tried to prevent it, Mexico won its independence.

5. ____

6. ____

Main Idea: The actions of General Santa Anna eventually led to the independence of Texas.

7. ____

8. ____

B. Reviewing Key Terms

Define or identify the following terms.

9. Great Plains ____

10. nomad ____

11. presidio ____

12. Texas War for Independence ______________________________________

13. Battle of the Alamo ____

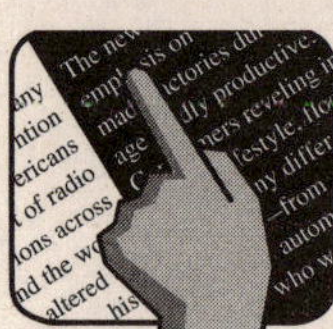

GUIDED READING AND REVIEW

Inventions and Innovations

A. AS YOU READ

As you read Section 1, fill in facts and details about developments in the United States during the early 1800s.

The Industrial Revolution
1. British technology spreads to the U.S. textile industry:
2. Eli Whitney's revolutionary concept changes industry forever:
3. The cotton gin has a significant impact on the United States:
Transportation
4. Robert Fulton improves river transportation:
5. Railroads are used to transport goods and people:
Manufacturing and Banking
6. Centralized workplaces increase production:
7. Banks help the economy grow:

B. REVIEWING KEY TERMS

Briefly define each of the following terms.

8. Industrial Revolution ____

9. manufacturing ____

10. free enterprise system ____

11. investment capital ____

12. bank note ____

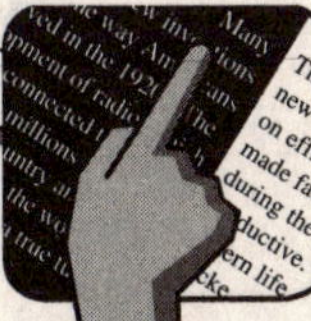

The Northern Section

A. AS YOU READ

Write in the missing cause or effect as you read Section 2.

1. Cause: _______________________	**1. Effect:** Grain crops were quickly used, transported, or converted into products that could be stored.
2. Cause: Francis Cabot Lowell built a centralized textile mill in Massachusetts.	**2. Effect:** _______________________
3. Cause: _______________________	**3. Effect:** Most early factory workers were women.
4. Cause: The populations of cities grew rapidly.	**4. Effect:** _______________________
5. Cause: Employers did not respond to workers' complaints about long hours and low pay.	**5. Effect:** _______________________

Write a sentence pair describing a cause-and-effect relationship in the 1800s.

6. Cause: _______________________	**6. Effect:** _______________________

B. REVIEWING KEY TERMS

Answer the questions below on the back of this paper or on a separate paper.

7. What were the two main *sections* of the United States in the early 1800s?

8. How did the population density of *urban* areas change as a result of *industrialization*?

9. Why did people live in *tenements*?

GUIDED READING AND REVIEW

The Southern Section

A. AS YOU READ

As you read Section 3, answer the following questions on the lines provided.

1. Why did southerners often say that "cotton is king"?

____

____

2. As northern urban areas developed, what happened in the South?

____

____

3. How were southern and northern cities alike, and how were they different?

____

____

4. What were the main differences between a slave's life on a small farm and on a plantation?

____

____

5. What was Denmark Vesey's plan?

____

____

6. What laws did Virginia and North Carolina pass in response to the slave rebellions?

____

____

B. REVIEWING KEY TERMS

Use each of the following in a sentence that suggests its meaning.

7. cotton belt ____

8. Turner's Rebellion ____

The Growth of Nationalism

A. AS YOU READ

All of the following sentences are incorrect. As you read Section 4, rewrite each sentence to make it correct.

1. Congress passed a tax on U.S. goods in 1816 to encourage Americans to buy foreign goods.

____

2. Under the Monroe Doctrine, the United States promised to play an active role in European affairs and assist in the further colonization of the Western Hemisphere.

____

3. Unlike many other prominent men of their times, Henry Clay, John C. Calhoun, and Andrew Jackson all refused to own slaves.

____

4. John Quincy Adams and Henry Clay clashed over such issues as protective tariffs and legislation authorizing public improvements.

____

5. Voters found few differences in the views of the candidates in the 1828 election.

____

6. Voter turnout decreased in 1828, which helped Adams.

____

B. REVIEWING KEY TERMS

Describe the main impact of each of the following.

7. *Dartmouth College* v. *Woodward* _________________________________

8. *McCulloch* v. *Maryland* ____

9. *Gibbons* v. *Ogden* ____

10. Monroe Doctrine ____

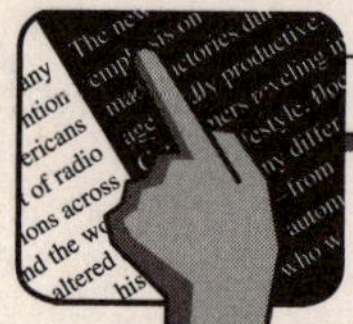

GUIDED READING AND REVIEW

The Age of Jackson

A. AS YOU READ

As you read Section 5, draw a line through the term or name in each group that is not related to the others. Explain how the remaining terms or names are related.

1. patronage   spoils system   Daniel Webster   Andrew Jackson

____

____

2. Tariff of 1828   South Carolina   Maysville, Kentucky   secede

____

____

3. Cherokees   Trail of Tears   Indian Removal Act   Robert Hayne

____

____

4. Henry Clay   Nicholas Biddle   Daniel Webster   Whigs

____

____

5. William Henry Harrison   Tariff of Abominations   Panic of 1837   Martin Van Buren

____

____

B. REVIEWING KEY TERMS

Use each pair of terms in a sentence.

6. patronage, spoils system _________________________________

____

7. Tariff of 1828, secede _________________________________

____

8. Indian Removal Act, Trail of Tears _________________________

____

Reforming Society

A. AS YOU READ

As you read Section 1, complete the chart below about the reform movements, their goals, and the leaders or organizations behind them.

Reform Movement	Leaders/Organizations	Goals
1. Protestant Revivalists		
2. Transcendentalism		
3. Temperance Movement		
4. Public Education Reform		
5. Prison Reform		
6. Utopian Communities		

B. REVIEWING KEY TERMS

Identify the following terms.

7. transcendentalism ____

8. temperance movement ____

9. abstinence ____

10. segregate ____

11. utopian community ____

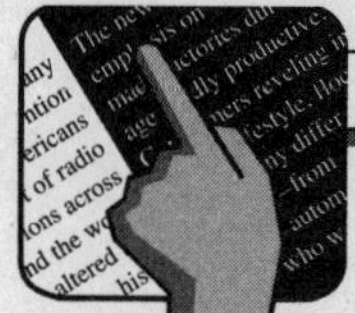

GUIDED READING AND REVIEW

The Antislavery Movement

A. As You Read

Below are four main ideas from Section 2. As you read, fill in two supporting details under each main idea.

Main Idea: Abolitionism had roots in early protests against slavery.

1. ____

2. ____

Main Idea: In the early 1800s some antislavery advocates supported the idea of colonization.

3. ____

4. ____

Main Idea: During the 1830s the antislavery movement became more aggressive, and some divisions appeared.

5. ____

6. ____

Main Idea: The abolitionist movement provoked opposition in both the North and the South.

7. ____

8. ____

B. Reviewing Key Terms

Identify each of the following and explain how it relates to the story of slavery in the early 1800s.

9. abolitionist movement ____

____

10. emancipation ____

____

11. Underground Railroad ____

____

12. gag rule ____

____

The Movement for Women's Rights

A. AS YOU READ

Complete each cause-and-effect sentence as you read Section 3.

1. Teaching was considered a proper occupation for a woman, *because*

____

____

2. *As a result of* women becoming more educated, they became more and more

dissatisfied with ____

____

3. *As a result of* fighting for the abolition of slavery, many women discovered that

____

____

4. Women delegates attending the first World Anti-Slavery Convention in

London were angry *because* ____

____

5. *Because of* their treatment at the World Anti-Slavery Convention, Lucretia

Mott and Elizabeth Cady Stanton ____

____

6. *As a result of* expanding educational opportunities, by the 1890s _______________

____

7. Few African American women attended women's rights conventions *because*

____

____

B. REVIEWING KEY TERMS

Answer each of the following questions.

8. What was the *Seneca Falls Convention,* and what impact did it have on the

movement for women's rights? ____

____

9. Why was *suffrage* such an important issue for women? _______________________

____

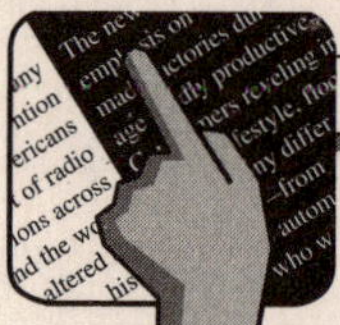

Growing Divisions

A. AS YOU READ

As you read Section 4, answer the following questions on the lines provided.

1. Why did immigrants settle in the North and West rather than in the South?

____

____

2. How did immigrants in the 1830s and 1840s differ culturally from native-born Americans?

____

____

3. Why did labor unions see the arrival of Irish immigrants as a threat?

____

____

4. How did the immigrants' religion lead to tension?

____

____

5. How did North-South tensions lead to splits in churches?

____

____

6. How did the reform movements clash with southern traditions?

____

____

B. REVIEWING KEY TERMS

Write a brief paragraph about Irish immigrants, using the terms *Irish Potato Famine, naturalized,* and *discrimination.*

7. ____

____

____

____

____

____

Two Nations

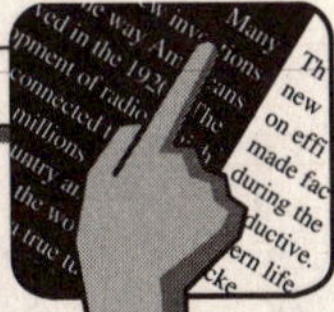

A. As You Read

Below are four main ideas from Section 1. As you read, fill in two supporting facts under each main idea.

Main Idea: Historians are divided over the extent of the differences that existed between the North and the South before the Civil War.

1. ____

2. ____

Main Idea: *Uncle Tom's Cabin* stirred northerners' fear that slavery threatened northern values.

3. ____

4. ____

Main Idea: Southerners justified slavery and attacked evils they saw in the North.

5. ____

6. ____

Main Idea: Differences in how the North and South had developed widened the gulf between the two regions.

7. ____

8. ____

B. Reviewing Key Terms

Define or identify each of the following terms, and explain how it relates to the section's content.

9. Union ____

____

10. prejudice ____

____

11. obsolete ____

____

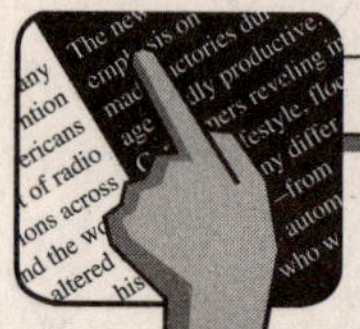

GUIDED READING AND REVIEW

The Mexican War and Slavery Extension

A. As You Read

As you read Section 2, answer the following questions on the lines provided.

1. Why did Americans disagree over the annexation of Texas? _______________________

____

2. Aside from the issue of annexation, what dispute caused tension between the
United States and Mexico? ____

____

3. What was the Bear Flag Revolt? ____

____

4. What events caused the Mexican government to want to end the Mexican War? __________

____

5. What land did the United States gain through the Treaty of Guadalupe
Hidalgo? ____

____

6. What were the effects of the Mexican War? ____

____

B. Reviewing Key Terms

Define or identify each of the following terms.

7. manifest destiny ____

____

8. annex ____

____

9. Gadsden Purchase ____

____

10. Wilmot Proviso ____

____

New Political Parties

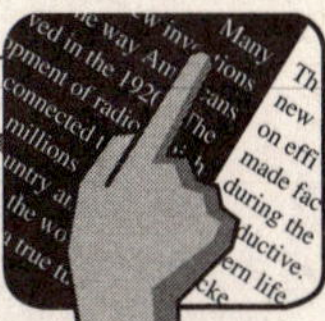

A. AS YOU READ

Complete each of the following sentences as you read Section 3.

1. The Missouri Compromise of 1820 failed to settle the issue of ________________________________

____

2. In the Compromise of 1850, Congress balanced the interests of the two
sections by ____

____

3. John C. Calhoun believed that control of the government by the North
threatened ____

____

4. The Whig party fell apart during the 1850s because ____________________________

____

5. The American party, or Know-Nothings, pledged to work for ________________________

____

____

6. The Kansas-Nebraska Act allowed the people of a territory to ______________________

____

____

7. As a result of Congress's passage of the Kansas-Nebraska Act, ____________________

____

8. The Republican party gained support among ____________________________________

____

B. REVIEWING KEY TERMS

Define or identify the following terms.

9. Compromise of 1850 ____

10. Fugitive Slave Act ____

11. nativism ____

12. Kansas-Nebraska Act ____

13. popular sovereignty ____

GUIDED READING AND REVIEW

The System Fails

A. AS YOU READ

As you read Section 4, draw a line through the term or name in each group that is not related to the others. Explain how the remaining terms or names are related.

1. Emigrant Aid societies   Kansas   New Englanders   Charles Sumner

____

____

2. Robert E. Lee   John Brown   "Bleeding Kansas"   Pottawatomie Creek

____

____

3. Roger Taney   Lecompton   *Scott* v. *Sandford*   Fifth Amendment

____

____

4. Illinois   Abraham Lincoln   Topeka   Stephen Douglas

____

____

5. James Buchanan   Harpers Ferry   John Brown   Robert E. Lee

____

____

B. REVIEWING KEY TERMS

Explain how each of the following terms relates to the section content.

6. free soiler ____

____

7. *Scott* v. *Sandford* _______________________________________

____

8. arsenal ____

____

A Nation Divided

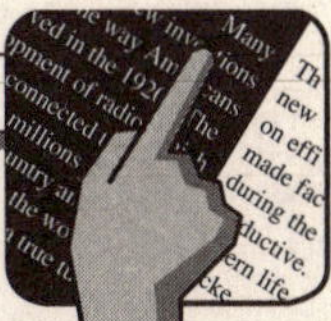

A. AS YOU READ

As you read Section 5, check the sentence in each group that is not related to
the other sentences. Then write another related sentence on the line provided.

GROUP 1

______ **a.** Abraham Lincoln won the presidency with only 39 percent of the popular vote.

______ **b.** Abraham Lincoln received no electoral votes from the South.

______ **c.** The Republicans, worried that William Henry Seward's antislavery views were too
extreme, nominated Abraham Lincoln as their candidate.

______ **d.** Democrats in the Lower South split with northern Democrats in 1860.

____

GROUP 2

______ **a.** Led by South Carolina, states in the Lower South left the Union.

______ **b.** Maryland, Delaware, Kentucky, and Missouri were known as the Border States.

______ **c.** The states that seceded formed a new nation called the Confederate States of America.

______ **d.** Secessionists argued that because the states had freely joined the Union, they could
freely leave it.

____

GROUP 3

______ **a.** The Constitutional Union party nominated John Bell, a moderate slaveholder.

______ **b.** Federal troops occupied Fort Sumter, even though South Carolina had seceded from
the Union.

______ **c.** Confederate troops took Fort Sumter by force.

______ **d.** Following the fall of Fort Sumter, the states of the Upper South joined the Confederacy.

____

B. REVIEWING KEY TERMS

Identify the states in each of the following parts of the Confederacy.

4. Lower South ____

5. Upper South ____

GUIDED READING AND REVIEW   **SECTION 1**

From Bull Run to Antietam

A. AS YOU READ

Write in the missing cause or effect as you read Section 1.

1. Cause: As Union forces began to retreat during the First Battle of Bull Run, a trainload of fresh Confederate troops arrived.	**1. Effect:** _______________________________ _______________________________ _______________________________
2. Cause: _______________________________ _______________________________ _______________________________	**2. Effect:** Confederate leaders persuaded most southern planters to stop exporting cotton.
3. Cause: _______________________________ _______________________________ _______________________________	**3. Effect:** The Union nearly succeeded in splitting the Confederacy in two.
4. Cause: Lee hoped a Confederate victory on Union soil would win European support for the South and turn northerners against the war.	**4. Effect:** _______________________________ _______________________________ _______________________________

B. REVIEWING KEY TERMS

Define or identify each of the following terms.

5. Civil War ____

6. casualty ____

7. war of attrition ____

Distinguish between the terms in each of the following groups.

8. shell, canister ____

____

9. First Battle of Bull Run, Battle of Shiloh, Battle of Antietam _______________

____

____

SECTION 2 | **GUIDED READING AND REVIEW**

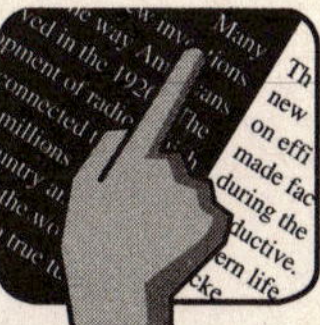

Life Behind the Lines

A. AS YOU READ

Below are three main ideas from Section 2. As you read, fill in two supporting facts under each main idea.

Main Idea: The Confederate government had to gather revenue, raise troops, and overcome the independence of its member states.

1. ____

2. ____

Main Idea: During the Civil War, the federal government passed laws that had a lasting impact on the nation.

3. ____

4. ____

Main Idea: Lincoln widened the goal of the Civil War from preserving the Union to emancipating enslaved people.

5. ____

6. ____

B. REVIEWING KEY TERMS

Explain how each of the following was related to the Civil War era.

7. draft ____

____

8. recognition ____

____

9. greenback ____

____

10. Copperheads ____

____

11. martial law ____

____

12. writ of *habeas corpus* ____

____

13. contraband ____

GUIDED READING AND REVIEW   SECTION 3

The Tide of War Turns

A. AS YOU READ

As you read Section 3, fill in the missing information about two important
Civil War battles.

GETTYSBURG
1. Strategic importance:
2. Geographic features:
3. Confederates' battle plan:
4. Reasons plan failed:

VICKSBURG
5. Strategic importance:
6. Geographic features:
7. Grant's failed attempts to take the city:
8. Grant's successful plan:

B. REVIEWING KEY TERMS

Answer the following questions.

9. How were the Battles of Fredericksburg and Chancellorsville similar?

____

10. What was the significance of the Gettysburg Address? _______________

____

SECTION 4 | **GUIDED READING AND REVIEW**

Devastation and New Freedom

A. AS YOU READ

As you read Section 4, answer the following questions on the lines provided.

1. What strategy did General Grant, as commander of the Union forces, hope to follow?

____

____

2. What strategy did General Sherman use after leaving Atlanta?

____

____

3. What event changed voters' minds about supporting Lincoln in the 1864 election?

____

____

4. How did voters and Congress show that they accepted Lincoln's stand against slavery?

____

____

5. Why did Lee finally surrender to Grant?

____

____

6. How was Lincoln assassinated?

____

____

B. REVIEWING KEY TERMS

Answer the following questions.

7. Explain how the *Battle of the Wilderness*, the *Battle of Spotsylvania*, and the *Battle of Cold Harbor* were related.

____

8. What was the significance of the *Thirteenth Amendment*? _______________________________

____

9. Why did Lee decide that his troops would not continue fighting as *guerrillas*?

____

____

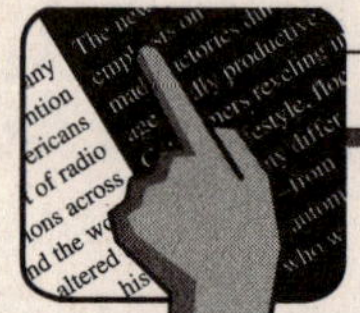

GUIDED READING AND REVIEW   SECTION 1

Presidential Reconstruction

A. As You Read

Below are four main ideas from Section 1. As you read, fill in three supporting facts under each main idea.

Main Idea: The Civil War took a huge physical and human toll on the South.

1. ____

2. ____

3. ____

Main Idea: Three major groups of people faced hardships and fears.

4. ____

5. ____

6. ____

Main Idea: Johnson's presidential Reconstruction plan was fairly generous to the South.

7. ____

8. ____

9. ____

Main Idea: Newly freed slaves celebrated their new freedom.

10. ____

11. ____

12. ____

B. Reviewing Key Terms

Explain the relation of each of the following terms to President Johnson.

13. Reconstruction ____

14. pardon ____

SECTION 2 | **GUIDED READING AND REVIEW**

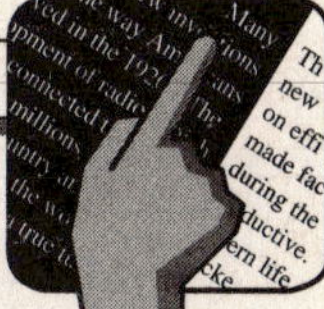

Congressional Reconstruction

A. As You Read

As you read Section 2, fill in the boxes in the sequence chain to show the series of events that led to the Fourteenth and Fifteenth amendments.

1. One by one, southern states met Johnson's Reconstruction demands and were restored to the Union.

2.

3.

4.

5.

6.

7.

8.

9.

B. Reviewing Key Terms

Define or identify each of the following terms.

10. black codes ____

11. civil rights ____

12. impeach ____

13. carpetbaggers ____

14. scalawags ____

GUIDED READING AND REVIEW | SECTION 3

Birth of the "New South"

A. AS YOU READ
As you read Section 3, answer the following questions on the lines provided.

1. Why did planters have difficulty finding people to work for them?

____

____

2. Why did sharecroppers rejoice at the chance to become tenant farmers?

____

____

3. How did the South experience some success by modeling itself after
the North?

____

____

4. Did Reconstruction transform the South into an industrialized, urban region
like the North? Explain.

____

____

5. How did some southern states use Reconstruction funds in beneficial ways?

____

____

6. Where did most of the Reconstruction funds come from? Where was a lot of
this money lost?

____

____

B. REVIEWING KEY TERMS
Define or identify each of the following terms.

7. sharecropping ____

8. tenant farming ____

9. infrastructure ____

SECTION 4 | **GUIDED READING AND REVIEW**

The End of Reconstruction

A. As You Read

Complete each of the following sentences as you read Section 4.

1. *Because* southerners felt a mixture of rage and fear about the Confederacy's defeat and the freedom of black southerners,

____

____

2. *Because* northerners expressed outrage at the violence of the Ku Klux Klan,

____

____

3. *Because* federal troops eventually withdrew from the South,

____

____

4. *As a result of* the widespread corruption in Grant's administration,

____

____

5. *As a result of* the Supreme Court's narrow interpretation of the Fourteenth and Fifteenth amendments in the 1870s,

____

____

6. *Because* the special congressional commission set up to resolve the election crisis of 1876 had a majority of Republicans,

____

____

B. Reviewing Key Terms

Identify each of the following and explain its significance.

7. solid South ____

____

____

8. Compromise of 1877 ____

____

____

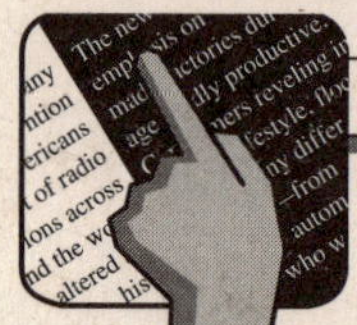

GUIDED READING AND REVIEW | **SECTION 1**

A Technological Revolution

A. AS YOU READ

Complete the chart below as you read Section 1. Fill in the name of the inventor, and list the advantages or benefits of each invention.

INVENTION/IDEA	INVENTOR/DEVELOPER	BENEFIT(S)
1. oil well, drill, and pump		
2. electric power and light bulb		
3. alternating current and transformers		
4. telegraphy		
5. telephone		
6. Bessemer process		

B. REVIEWING KEY TERMS

Define or identify each of the following terms.

7. patent ____

8. productivity ____

9. transcontinental railroad ____

10. mass production ____

SECTION 2 | **GUIDED READING AND REVIEW**

The Growth of Big Business

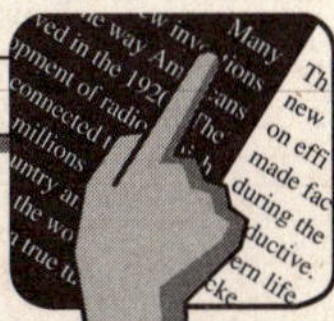

A. AS YOU READ

Below are four main ideas from Section 2. As you read, fill in two supporting details under each main idea.

Main Idea: Powerful industrialists who established large businesses in the late 1800s have been described as "captains of industry" and as "robber barons."

1. ____

2. ____

Main Idea: In the late 1800s, the theory of social Darwinism arose.

3. ____

4. ____

Main Idea: Industrialists such as Andrew Carnegie and John D. Rockefeller used varied forms of industrial control to lower production costs and drive out competition.

5. ____

6. ____

Main Idea: In 1890, Congress made an attempt to restrict big business, but it was not effective.

7. ____

8. ____

B. REVIEWING KEY TERMS

Define or identify each of the following terms.

9. oligopoly ____

10. monopoly ____

11. cartel ____

12. vertical consolidation ____

13. economies of scale ____

14. horizontal consolidation ____

15. trust ____

16. Sherman Antitrust Act ____

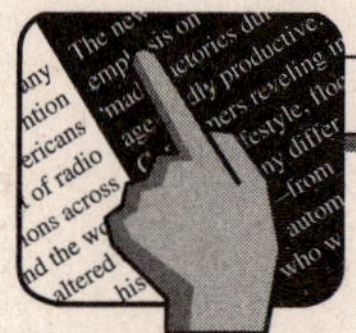

Industrialization and Workers

A. AS YOU READ

Complete each sentence below as you read Section 3.

1. Some 14 million people immigrated to America between 1860 and 1900 *because*

____

____

2. During the late 1800s, millions of Americans moved from farms to cities *because*

____

____

3. Factory laborers resented the introduction of methods to improve efficiency

because ____

____

4. Factory managers referred to workers as "hands" or "operatives" *because*

____

____

5. Fires and accidents were common occurrences in factories *because* ___________________

____

6. Despite harsh working conditions, there was no shortage of labor in America

because ____

____

7. Many children had to go to work in the 1880s *because*

____

____

8. In the late 1800s, families in need of food, clothing, and shelter often went

without these basics *because* ____

____

B. REVIEWING KEY TERMS

9. The system of *piecework* caused some workers to earn more than others *because* ___________

____

10. The *division of labor* took much of the joy out of work, but owners liked it

because ____

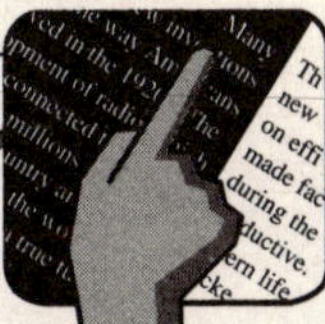

The Great Strikes

A. As You Read

As you read Section 4, cross out the term or name in each group that is not
related to the others. Then explain how the remaining terms or names are related.

1. socialism   Karl Marx   National Trades Union   *Communist Manifesto*

____

____

2. Terence Powderley   Wobblies   Knights of Labor   social reforms

____

____

3. skilled workers   Samuel Gompers   miners   American Federation of Labor

____

____

4. Rutherford B. Hayes   railroad strike   Pittsburgh   Andrew Carnegie

____

____

5. Pinkertons   Haymarket   Homestead Strike   Henry Frick

____

____

6. American Railway Union   Eugene V. Debs   Pullman Strike   Alexander Berkman

____

____

B. Reviewing Key Terms

Define or identify each of the following terms.

7. socialism ____

8. collective bargaining _____________________________________

9. scabs ____

10. anarchists ____

GUIDED READING AND REVIEW   SECTION 1

Moving West

A. AS YOU READ

As you read Section 1, answer the following questions.

1. What push factors urged settlers toward the West? _______________________________

____

2. What federal actions paved the way for western migration in the 1860s? _____________

____

3. What legal incentive drew settlers westward? _____________________________________

____

4. How did western settlement expand from mainly white easterners to a more
diverse population? ____

____

5. Why were thousands of African Americans eager to move westward? _________________

____

B. REVIEWING KEY TERMS

Explain the role played by each of the following in the settlement of the West.

6. push-pull factors ____

____

7. Morrill Land-Grant Act ____

____

8. land speculator ____

____

9. Homestead Act ____

____

10. Exodusters ____

____

SECTION 2 | **GUIDED READING AND REVIEW**

Conflict with Native Americans

A. AS YOU READ

As you read Section 2, write one or two sentences to support each of the following main ideas.

Main Idea: The introduction of horses had a significant impact on Native Americans.

1. ____

____

Main Idea: Cycles of revenge grew out of clashes between Native Americans and settlers over land and resources.

2. ____

____

Main Idea: As American settlers pushed westward, many Indian nations were weakened or destroyed.

3. ____

____

Main Idea: The government and many reformers believed that Indians should be "civilized."

4. ____

____

Main Idea: Parts of Indian Territory were eventually opened up to settlers.

5. ____

____

B. REVIEWING KEY TERMS

Define or identify each of the following terms.

6. reservation ____

7. Battle of Little Bighorn ____

8. Massacre at Wounded Knee ______________________________________

9. Dawes Act ____

10. boomers ____

11. sooners ____

GUIDED READING AND REVIEW | SECTION 3

Mining, Ranching, and Farming

A. As You Read

As you read Section 3, fill in facts and details about mining, ranching, and farming in the American West.

MINING
1. Impact of gold strikes:
2. Events after easily gathered gold was gone:

RANCHING
3. Causes of cattle boom:
4. Realities of cowboy life:

FARMING
5. Hardships:
6. Improvements in machinery, technology, and farming techniques:

B. Reviewing Key Terms

Use each of the following terms in a sentence that suggests its meaning.

7. placer mining ____

8. long drive ____

9. dry farming ____

SECTION 4 | **GUIDED READING AND REVIEW**

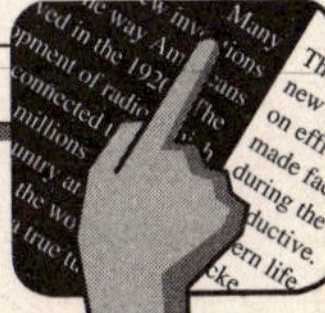

Populism

A. AS YOU READ

As you read Section 4, check the sentence in each group that is not related to the other sentences. Then write another related sentence on the lines provided.

GROUP 1

_____ **a.** Competition from foreign growers hurt American farmers.

_____ **b.** Farmers wanted the federal government to stop raising tariffs.

_____ **c.** The Grange helped farmers form cooperatives.

_____ **d.** Tariffs reduced the international market for American farm products.

____

GROUP 2

_____ **a.** Deflation helped people who lent out money.

_____ **b.** Farmers' Alliances launched harsh attacks on monopolies.

_____ **c.** After the Civil War, the nation experienced a long period of falling prices.

_____ **d.** People who borrow money benefit from inflation.

____

GROUP 3

_____ **a.** The platform of the People's party called for unlimited minting of silver.

_____ **b.** In the 1892 presidential election, James B. Weaver won barely a million votes.

_____ **c.** During its first decade, enforcement of the Sherman Antitrust Act was lax.

_____ **d.** The Populists sought a united front of African American and white farmers.

____

B. REVIEWING KEY TERMS

Define or identify each of the following terms.

4. monetary policy ____

5. Bland-Allison Act ____

6. Interstate Commerce Act ____

7. Cross of Gold speech ____

Politics in the Gilded Age

A. AS YOU READ

As you read Section 1, write one or two sentences to support each of the following main ideas.

1. In the late 1800s most Americans, in theory, supported a laissez-faire approach to economic matters. ____

____

2. After Congress awarded the Union Pacific Railroad loans and land for the transcontinental railroad, a notorious scandal occurred. ____

____

3. The spoils system had negative consequences for American politics. ____

____

4. During the Gilded Age, sharp differences existed between Republicans and Democrats on major issues. ____

____

5. Political leaders tried to reform the spoils system in the late 1800s. ____

____

6. Government officials tried but failed to regulate the railroads. ____

____

B. REVIEWING KEY TERMS

Explain how each of the following terms relates to the post-Reconstruction era in the United States.

7. Gilded Age ____

8. laissez-faire ____

9. subsidy ____

10. blue laws ____

11. civil service ____

12. Pendleton Civil Service Act ____

13. *Munn v. Illinois* ____

SECTION 2 | **GUIDED READING AND REVIEW**

People on the Move

A. AS YOU READ

As you read Section 2, complete the following sentences.

1. In the late 1800s, people from all over the world fled their homelands *because*

____

____

2. Beginning in 1892, some immigrants to the United States were denied admission *because*

____

____

3. Many European immigrants settled near ports of entry and inland cities
because _______________________________________

____

4. Very few immigrants settled in the South *because* _____________________

____

5. Asian immigrants were often targets of suspicion, hostility, and discrimination
because _______________________________________

____

6. Chinese immigrants tended to live in their own ethnic communities *because* _______________

____

7. In the early 1900s, many Mexicans immigrated to southwestern lands *because*

____

____

B. REVIEWING KEY TERMS

Define or identify each of the following terms.

8. pogroms ____________________________________

9. steerage ___________________________________

10. quarantine _________________________________

11. Chinese Exclusion Act ______________________

12. Gentlemen's Agreement ______________________

13. alien _____________________________________

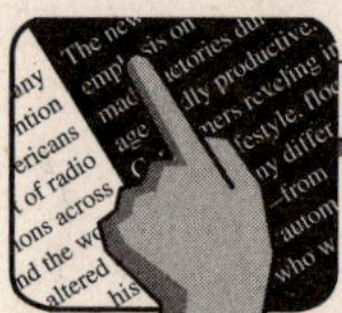

GUIDED READING AND REVIEW   SECTION 3

The Challenge of the Cities

A. As You Read

As you read Section 3, write in the missing cause or effect.

1. Cause: Factories produced goods formerly made by farm women, and new machines reduced the need for manual labor.

1. Effect: ____

____

____

2. Cause: ____

____

____

2. Effect: African Americans moved from rural areas to cities.

3. Cause: The use of trolleys, subways, automobiles, and elevators became widespread.

3. Effect: ____

____

____

4. Cause: ____

____

____

4. Effect: Old urban residential neighborhoods gradually declined.

5. Cause: The middle and upper classes began moving to the suburbs.

5. Effect: ____

____

____

B. Reviewing Key Terms

Define or identify each of the following terms.

6. suburb ____

7. tenement ____

8. political machine ____

9. graft ____

SECTION 4 | **GUIDED READING AND REVIEW**

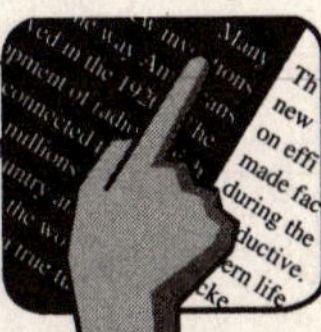

Ideas for Reform

A. AS YOU READ

As you read Section 4, draw a line through the term or name in each group that is
not related to the others. Explain how the remaining terms or names are related.

1. social gospel movement   Jewish synagogues   Hull House   Federal Council of the Churches of Christ

____

____

____

2. Frances Willard   Ellen Gates Starr   Jane Addams   Lillian Wald

____

____

____

3. Immigration Restriction League   American Protective Association   nativism   Charity Organization Society

____

____

____

4. Anti-Saloon League   Chinese Exclusion Act   Prohibition party   Woman's Christian Temperance Union

____

____

____

B. REVIEWING KEY TERMS

Use each of the following terms in a sentence that suggests its meaning.

5. settlement house ___________________________________

6. temperance movement ___________________________________

7. prohibition ___________________________________

8. vice ___________________________________

GUIDED READING AND REVIEW | SECTION 1

The Expansion of Education

A. As You Read

As you read Section 1, complete each of the following sentences.

1. By 1900 children's attendance at school had become a legal requirement in
31 states, *because* ____

____

____

2. Many immigrants considered education important, *because* ______________

____

3. Some immigrants sent their children to religious schools that taught in their

native language, *because* ____

____

4. Not everyone benefited equally from public education, *because* ______________

____

5. College enrollment more than doubled between 1890 and 1900, *because* ______________

____

____

6. W.E.B. Du Bois rejected Booker T. Washington's suggestion that African
Americans should focus on building economic security through vocational
studies, *because* ____

____

____

B. Reviewing Key Terms

Define or identify each of the following terms.

7. literacy ____

8. assimilation ____

9. philanthropists ____

10. Niagara Movement ____

SECTION 2 | **GUIDED READING AND REVIEW**

New Forms of Entertainment

A. AS YOU READ

As you read Section 2, write in the missing cause or effect.

<table>
<tr>
<td>1. Cause: At the turn of the century, workers began to have more leisure time and more money to spend on entertainment.</td>
<td>1. Effect: ____</td>
</tr>
<tr>
<td>2. Cause: ____</td>
<td>2. Effect: Professional sports were born when entrepreneurs began to charge admission to games.</td>
</tr>
<tr>
<td>3. Cause: New typesetting machinery enabled publishers to produce larger and more entertaining publications.</td>
<td>3. Effect: ____</td>
</tr>
<tr>
<td>4. Cause: Congress lowered postal rates for periodicals.</td>
<td>4. Effect: ____</td>
</tr>
<tr>
<td>5. Cause: ____</td>
<td>5. Effect: White audiences accepted African American spirituals, and a new form of spiritual became identified as an American art form.</td>
</tr>
</table>

B. REVIEWING KEY TERMS

Describe the origins of each of the following terms.

6. vaudeville ____

7. yellow journalism ____

8. ragtime ____

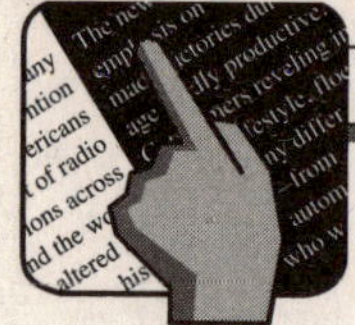

GUIDED READING AND REVIEW   SECTION 3

The World of Jim Crow

A. AS YOU READ

Below are three main ideas from Section 3. As you read, fill in three supporting facts under each main idea statement.

Main Idea: During the 1890s, southern states employed several tactics to deny African Americans the vote.

1. ____

2. ____

3. ____

Main Idea: In the South, society was organized according to the Jim Crow system.

4. ____

5. ____

6. ____

Main Idea: African Americans responded to discrimination in several ways.

7. ____

8. ____

9. ____

B. REVIEWING KEY TERMS

Identify how each of the following terms relates to the world of Jim Crow.

10. poll tax ____

____

11. grandfather clause ____

____

12. *Plessy* v. *Ferguson* ____

____

13. lynching ____

____

14. National Association for the Advancement of Colored People (NAACP)

____

____

SECTION 4 | **GUIDED READING AND REVIEW**

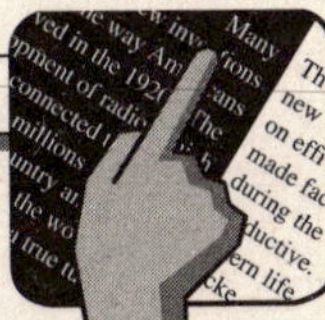

The Changing Role of Women

A. As You Read

As you read Section 4, answer the following questions.

1. What were the arguments on both sides of *the woman question*?

____

____

2. How did technological advances in the late 1800s change women's work in the home?

____

____

3. What advantages did department stores and mail-order catalogs have over general stores?

____

____

4. How did employers discriminate against women working outside the home?

____

____

5. How did women professionals fare in the working world?

____

____

6. How did women's clubs benefit the women who joined them?

____

____

7. In addition to economic and political rights, what other issues concerned women by the early 1900s?

____

____

B. Reviewing Key Terms

Define or identify each of the following terms.

8. department stores _________________________________

9. rural free delivery _________________________________

10. mail-order catalog _________________________________

The Pressure to Expand

A. AS YOU READ

As you read Section 1, check the sentence in each group that is not related to the other sentences. Then write another related sentence on the line provided.

GROUP 1

_____ **a.** Nationalism caused competition for empires among European nations.

_____ **b.** The growth of industry in Europe created an increased need for natural resources.

_____ **c.** George Washington advised Americans to avoid permanent alliances.

_____ **d.** Western nations believed that they had a duty to spread the blessings of their civilization.

____

GROUP 2

_____ **a.** Commodore Perry persuaded the Japanese to open trade with the United States.

_____ **b.** The United States focused its energies on settling the West.

_____ **c.** Secretary of State Seward sent troops to Mexico to force out the French.

_____ **d.** The United States wanted control of some of the Pacific Islands.

____

GROUP 3

_____ **a.** Many business leaders encouraged the expansion of American markets.

_____ **b.** Some Americans used the idea of social Darwinism to justify taking over new territories.

_____ **c.** Lobbyists pushed for a stronger navy to protect new foreign markets.

_____ **d.** The United States agreed to let Hawaii sell sugar in the United States tax free.

____

B. REVIEWING KEY TERMS

Explain how each of the following terms relates to expansionism in the late 1800s.

4. imperialism ____

5. nationalism ____

6. annex ____

7. banana republic ____

SECTION 2 | **GUIDED READING AND REVIEW**

The Spanish-American War

A. AS YOU READ

Below are three main ideas from Section 2. As you read, fill in two supporting details under each main idea.

Main Idea: In the 1890s, the United States asserted its power in diplomatic and military conflicts in Latin America.

1. ____

2. ____

Main Idea: Between 1898 and 1900 the United States acquired new territories and powers.

3. ____

4. ____

Main Idea: Growing trade with Asia prompted the United States to pursue U.S. interests in the Pacific.

5. ____

6. ____

B. REVIEWING KEY TERMS

Explain how each of the following terms relates to American expansion.

7. arbitration ____

____

____

8. jingoism ____

____

____

9. sphere of influence ____

____

____

10. Open Door Policy ____

____

____

GUIDED READING AND REVIEW | **SECTION 3**

A New Foreign Policy

A. AS YOU READ

As you read Section 3, answer the following questions on the lines provided.

1. How did the United States gain control of what would become the Panama Canal Zone?

____

____

2. What was the American reaction to President Roosevelt's securing of the Canal

Zone? ____

____

3. How did Roosevelt prevent European intervention in Santo Domingo?

____

____

4. Why did Roosevelt arrange a peace treaty between Russia and Japan?

____

____

5. How did President Taft's foreign policy goals compare with those of

Roosevelt? ____

____

6. How did American investments fare under "dollar diplomacy"?

____

____

B. REVIEWING KEY TERMS

Explain the significance of each of the following pairs in American foreign policy
in the early 1900s.

7. concession, Panama ____

____

8. Roosevelt Corollary, Theodore Roosevelt _______________________________________

____

9. "dollar diplomacy," William Howard Taft _______________________________________

____

SECTION 4 | **GUIDED READING AND REVIEW**

Debating America's New Role

A. As You Read

As you read Section 4, fill in the missing information about Americans' attitudes toward imperialism.

ANTI-IMPERIALISM
1. Moral and political arguments:
2. Racial arguments:
3. Economic arguments:

APPEAL OF IMPERIALISM
4. American "frontier" vision:
5. Economic and strategic arguments:

B. Reviewing Key Terms

Define or identify each of the following terms.

6. racism ____

7. compulsory ____

8. Great White Fleet ____

GUIDED READING AND REVIEW   SECTION 1

The Origins of Progressivism

A. As You Read

Below are four main ideas from Section 1. As you read, fill in at least two supporting facts under each main idea.

Main Idea: Although Progressives held different views, most reformers agreed on certain basic beliefs and goals.

1. ____

2. ____

Main Idea: Reform-minded writers greatly influenced public opinion.

3. ____

4. ____

Main Idea: Reform groups organized to speak out on social, economic, and political issues.

5. ____

6. ____

Main Idea: A number of women became prominent leaders in the labor reform movement.

7. ____

8. ____

B. Reviewing Key Terms

Define or identify each of the following terms.

9. Progressive Era ____

10. muckraker ____

11. injunction ____

SECTION 2 | **GUIDED READING AND REVIEW**

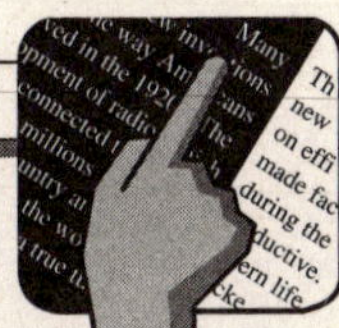

Progressive Legislation

A. AS YOU READ

Examine the progressive reform programs and actions below. As you read Section 2,
show the level of government at which each reform occurred by writing C for city,
S for state, or F for federal in the blank.

_____ 1. establishment of a Children's Bureau and a Women's Bureau

_____ 2. efforts to oust or work with political machines

_____ 3. abolition of child labor

_____ 4. use of government intervention to settle strikes

_____ 5. minimum wage and maximum hour legislation for women

_____ 6. preservation of national forest lands

_____ 7. provision of welfare services such as children's playgrounds, free
kindergartens, and lodging for the homeless

_____ 8. antitrust actions against holding companies

_____ 9. regulation or dislodging of public utilities monopolies

_____ 10. adoption of direct primaries

B. REVIEWING KEY TERMS

Define or identify each of the following terms.

11. direct primary ____

____

12. initiative ____

____

13. referendum ____

____

14. recall ____

____

15. holding company ____

____

Progressivism Under Taft and Wilson

A. As You Read

As you read Section 3, draw a line through the term or name in each group that is not related to the others. Explain how the remaining terms or names are related.

1. Ballinger-Pinchot affair   tariff   Progressives   public lands

____

____

2. New Nationalism   business regulation   income tax   Payne-Aldrich Tariff

____

____

3. Bull Moose platform   Mann-Elkins Act   women's suffrage   eight-hour workday

____

____

4. William Jennings Bryan   New Freedom   Woodrow Wilson   Democratic Party

____

____

5. Federal Trade   Federal Reserve   Socialist Party   Federal Farm
Commission   System   Loan Board

____

____

B. Reviewing Key Terms

Answer each of the following questions.

6. What did Theodore Roosevelt's *New Nationalism* program propose?

____

____

7. What was the general purpose of the *Clayton Antitrust Act?* _____________________

____

8. What was the *Federal Reserve System?* _____________________________________

____

SECTION 4 | **GUIDED READING AND REVIEW**

Suffrage at Last

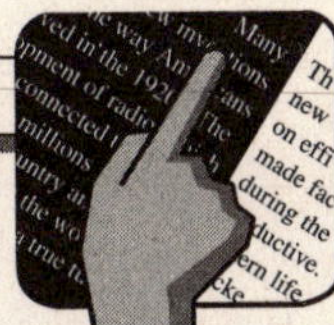

A. As You Read

As you read Section 4, complete each sentence on the lines provided.

1. The year 1848 was noteworthy for the suffrage movement *because*

____

____

2. Getting individual states to let women vote proved to be a successful approach to suffrage in the western states *because* _______________________

____

3. At the turn of the century, the suffrage movement stalled *because*

____

____

4. A split occurred in the suffrage movement when the NAWSA leadership expelled Alice Paul's Congressional Union *because* _______________________

____

5. In 1918 Congress passed the proposed suffrage amendment *because*

____

____

B. Reviewing Key Terms

Explain how each of the following terms relates to the story of women's suffrage.

6. civil disobedience ____

____

7. National American Woman Suffrage Association (NAWSA)

____

____

8. Congressional Union (CU) ____

____

GUIDED READING AND REVIEW | **SECTION 1**

The Road to War

A. AS YOU READ

As you read Section 1, complete the sequence chain below to show the series of events that led to World War I and shaped the American response to the war.

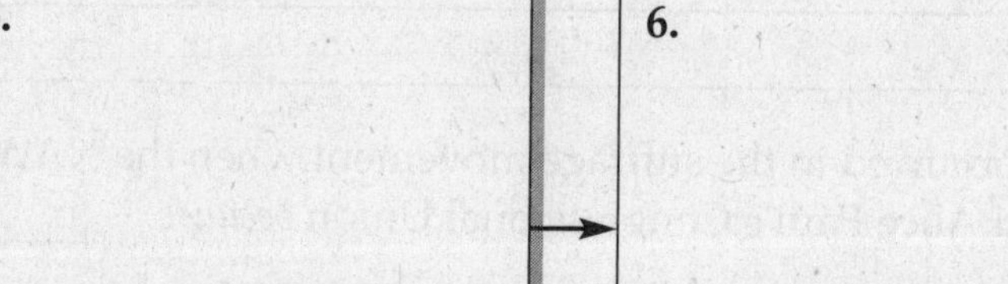

1. Archduke Francis Ferdinand and his wife Sophia are assassinated in Bosnia.	**2.**	**3.**

4.	**5.**	**6.**

7.	**8.**	**9.**

B. REVIEWING KEY TERMS

Answer each of the following questions.

10. How did *militarism* help start the Great War? ____

____

11. Which of the *Allies* began *mobilization* first? ____

____

12. Which of the *Central Powers* was led by an *autocrat*? ________________________________

____

13. What tactics did the two armies use to try to break the stalemate? ___________________

____

SECTION 2 **GUIDED READING AND REVIEW**

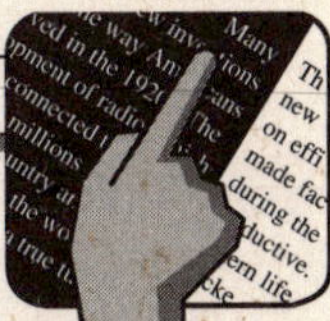

The United States Declares War

A. AS YOU READ

As you read Section 2, complete each of the following sentences on
the lines provided.

1. German submarine warfare pushed the United States toward war *because*

____

2. Americans received a pro-Allied version of war events in Europe *because*

____

3. President Wilson began to support the idea of war preparedness *because*

____

4. In February 1917, Wilson broke off diplomatic relations with Germany *because*

____

5. The Zimmermann note pushed the United States closer to war *because*

____

6. The Russian Revolution pushed the United States closer to war *because*

____

7. On March 20, 1917, Wilson's Cabinet voted unanimously for war *because*

____

B. REVIEWING KEY TERMS

Use each of the following terms in a sentence.

8. U-boat ____

____

9. Sussex pledge ____

____

10. Zimmermann note ____

____

11. Russian Revolution ____

____

GUIDED READING AND REVIEW | **SECTION 3**

Americans on the European Front

A. AS YOU READ

As you read Section 3, answer the following questions on the lines provided.

1. Why did Congress pass a Selective Service Act? ________________________________

____

2. Why was the convoy system established? ____________________________________

____

3. What divisions existed among Allied troops in Europe? ___________________________

____

4. How did Lenin's takeover of Russia affect German war strategy? ___________________

____

5. How did Americans help turn the tide of war and send the Germans into

retreat? ____

____

6. How did illness add to the death toll during the last months of the war? ____________

____

7. What was the cost of World War I in terms of lives? _____________________________

____

B. REVIEWING KEY TERMS

Define or identify each of the following terms.

8. Selective Service Act ____

9. American Expeditionary Force ____

10. convoy ____

11. armistice ____

12. genocide ____

SECTION 4 | **GUIDED READING AND REVIEW**

Americans on the Home Front

A. AS YOU READ

As you read Section 4, draw a line through the term or name in each group that is not related to the others. Explain how the remaining terms or names are related.

1. William Gibbs McAdoo	Liberty Bonds	Scouts	Henry Ford
2. War Trade Board	National Security League	National War Labor Board	War Industries Board
3. Lever Food and Fuel Control Act	censorship	Committee on Public Information	Sedition Act
4. Industrial Workers of the World	Eugene V. Debs	Socialists	Espionage Act
5. African Americans	Mexican Americans	Germans	women

B. REVIEWING KEY TERMS

Use each of the following terms in a sentence.

6. Liberty Bonds ____

7. price controls ____

8. rationing ____

9. daylight saving time ____

10. sedition ____

11. vigilante ____

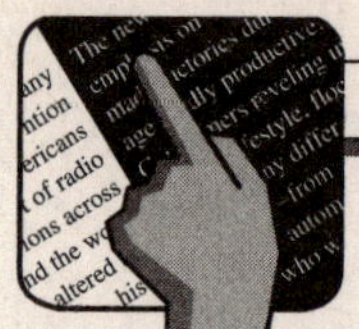

GUIDED READING AND REVIEW **SECTION 5**

Global Peacemaker

A. AS YOU READ

As you read Section 5, fill in two supporting details under each of the following main ideas.

Main Idea: At the Paris Peace Conference, President Wilson was forced to compromise on his vision for peace.

1. ____

2. ____

Main Idea: The proposal for a League of Nations produced resistance to the Versailles Treaty in the United States.

3. ____

4. ____

Main Idea: Several challenges faced Americans after the war, making the transition to peace difficult.

5. ____

6. ____

B. REVIEWING KEY TERMS

Explain how each of the following terms relates to postwar peacemaking.

7. Fourteen Points ____

____

8. self-determination ____

____

9. spoils ____

____

10. League of Nations ____

____

11. reparations ____

____

12. Versailles Treaty ____

____

SECTION 1 | **GUIDED READING AND REVIEW**

Society in the 1920s

A. AS YOU READ

As you read Section 1, answer the following questions on the lines provided.

1. Why is the flapper viewed as a symbol of the 1920s?

____

____

2. How did women's status at work and in politics change during the 1920s?

____

____

3. Why did large numbers of African Americans migrate from the South to the North during the early 1900s?

____

____

4. How did suburbs change during the 1920s?

____

____

5. Why did Charles Lindbergh become an American hero?

____

____

6. What other heroes inspired Americans during this decade?

____

____

B. REVIEWING KEY TERMS

Define or identify each of the following terms.

7. flapper ____

8. demographics ____

9. barrio ____

Mass Media and the Jazz Age

A. AS YOU READ

As you read Section 2, draw a line through the term or name in each group that is not related to the others. Explain how the remaining terms or names are related.

1. William Randolph Hearst   newspapers   Louis Armstrong   mass media

____

____

2. jazz   Harlem   Hollywood   Duke Ellington

____

____

3. *Rhapsody in Blue*   Sinclair Lewis   *Main Street*   Nobel Prize for Literature

____

____

4. Lost Generation   Gertrude Stein   Ernest Hemingway   George Gershwin

____

____

5. NAACP   Georgia O'Keeffe   Harlem Renaissance   James Weldon Johnson

____

____

B. REVIEWING KEY TERMS

Explain how each of the following terms relates to the 1920s.

6. mass media ____

7. Jazz Age ____

8. Lost Generation ____

9. Harlem Renaissance ____

SECTION 3 | **GUIDED READING AND REVIEW**

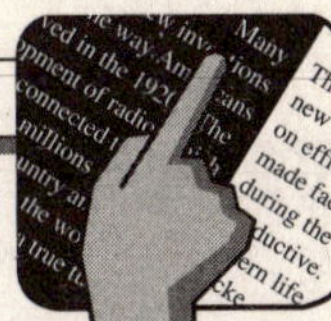

Cultural Conflicts

A. As You Read

As you read Section 3, complete the paragraphs by writing the correct answers in the blanks provided. Then write a title stating the main idea of the paragraphs.

Title: _______________________________________

Many Americans, believing that the country was on the road to moral and social decay, sought to slow down the pace of change that defined the 1920s. Prohibitionists had already achieved their goal with the ratification of the **(1)** _____________________ , which outlawed the manufacture, sale, and transportation of any intoxicating beverage. However, Prohibition proved impossible to enforce and led to illegal trafficking in liquor by **(2)** _____________________ , the most famous of which was Al Capone's, in Chicago.

In response to challenges to their religious principles, traditionalists published a set of beliefs that came to be called **(3)** _____________________ . Tennessee passed a law banning the teaching of **(4)** _____________________ , the theory that human beings and all other species developed over time from simple life forms. A biology teacher named **(5)** _____________________ decided to challenge the ban, so he had a friend file suit against him. The trial pitted **(6)** _____________________ , a lawyer famous for defending political and labor activists, against **(7)** _____________________ , a former presidential candidate who argued for the literal truth of the Bible.

Another group sought to curb change through violent means. An old enemy of racial harmony and an advocate of white supremacy, the **(8)** _____________________ launched a campaign of terror against African Americans, Catholics, Jews, and **(9)** _____________________ . Partly as a result of such continued violence, black leader **(10)** _____________________ urged African Americans to return to **(11)** _____________________ .

B. Reviewing Key Terms

Explain how the key terms in each pair are related.

12. bootlegger, speakeasy ____

____

13. fundamentalism, Scopes trial __________________________________

____

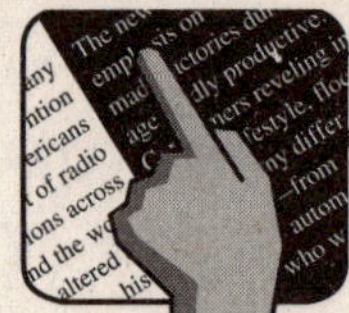

A Republican Decade

A. As You Read

As you read Section 1, fill in three supporting details under each of the following main ideas.

Main Idea: The establishment of communism in the Soviet Union produced a red scare in the United States.

1. ____

2. ____

3. ____

Main Idea: A rash of strikes in 1919 convinced many Americans that Communists were behind the labor unrest.

4. ____

5. ____

6. ____

Main Idea: The Republican Party dominated politics in the 1920s.

7. ____

8. ____

9. ____

B. Reviewing Key Terms

Define or identify each of the following terms.

10. isolationism ____

11. disarmament ____

12. quota ____

13. Teapot Dome Scandal _________________________________

14. Kellogg-Briand Pact _________________________________

SECTION 2 | **GUIDED READING AND REVIEW**

A Business Boom

A. AS YOU READ

As you read Section 2, fill in two supporting details under each of the following main ideas.

Main Idea: The development of a consumer economy changed American life.

1. ____

2. ____

Main Idea: Henry Ford strived to manufacture automobiles as efficiently as possible.

3. ____

4. ____

Main Idea: The growth in popularity of the automobile fueled the growth of related businesses.

5. ____

6. ____

B. REVIEWING KEY TERMS

Define each of the following terms, and explain the role each played in the business boom of the 1920s.

7. consumer economy ____

____

8. installment plan ____

____

9. assembly line ____

____

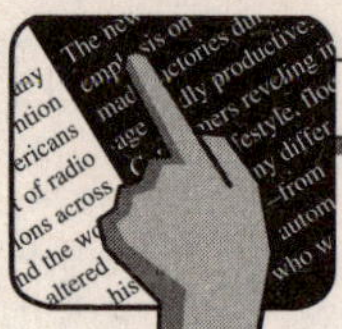

GUIDED READING AND REVIEW | **SECTION 3**

The Economy in the Late 1920s

A. AS YOU READ

As you read Section 3, draw a line through the term or name in each group that is not related to the others. Explain how the remaining terms or names are related.

1. rising stock values   rising wages   overproduction   low unemployment

____

____

2. Bruce Barton   Belle Moskowitz   Herbert Hoover   John J. Raskob

____

____

3. welfare capitalism   credit buying   speculation   "get-rich-quick" attitude

____

____

4. McNary-Haugen bill   prosperity   low crop prices   rural bank failures

____

____

5. medical advances   overproduction   uneven wealth   rising debt

____

____

B. REVIEWING KEY TERMS

Explain the following key terms.

6. welfare capitalism ____

7. speculation ____

8. buying on margin ____

GUIDED READING AND REVIEW

The Stock Market Crash

A. As You Read

As you read Section 1, fill in the boxes in the sequence chain below to show the ripple effects of the stock market crash.

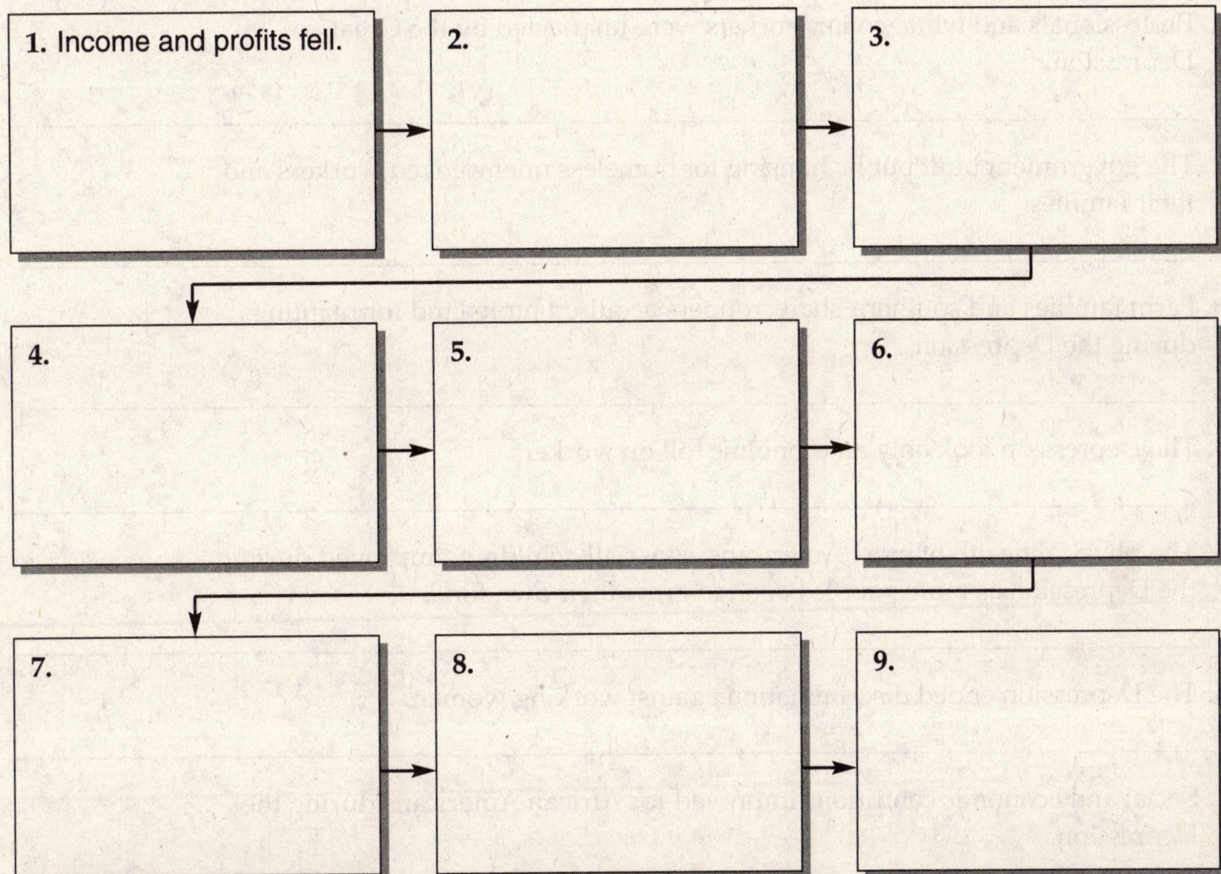

B. Reviewing Key Terms

Define or identify each of the following terms.

10. Dow-Jones Industrial Average ____

11. Black Tuesday ____

12. Great Crash ____

13. business cycle ____

14. Great Depression ____

GUIDED READING AND REVIEW   **SECTION 2**

Social Effects of the Depression

A. As You Read

All of the following sentences are incorrect. As you read Section 2, rewrite each sentence to make it correct.

1. Professionals and white-collar workers were unaffected by the Great Depression.

____

2. The government built public housing for homeless unemployed workers and their families.

____

3. Farm families and southern sharecroppers acquired more land for planting during the Depression.

____

4. The Depression took only an economic toll on workers.

____

5. The physical health of most Americans, especially children, improved during the Depression as more people began to grow their own food.

____

6. The Depression ended discrimination against working women.

____

7. Social and economic conditions improved for African Americans during the Depression.

____

B. Reviewing Key Terms

Identify the following terms, and explain how each term relates to the Great Depression.

8. Hoovervilles ____

9. Dust Bowl ____

SECTION 3 | **GUIDED READING AND REVIEW**

Surviving the Great Depression

A. AS YOU READ

As you read Section 3, check the sentence in each group that is not related to the other sentences. Then write another related sentence on the line provided.

GROUP 1

_____ **a.** Tenant groups formed to protest rent increases and evictions.

_____ **b.** Many Americans avoided buying on credit.

_____ **c.** Americans pulled together to help each other.

_____ **d.** People helped those they saw as worse off than themselves.

____

GROUP 2

_____ **a.** Some Americans supported radical and reform movements.

_____ **b.** The infant son of Charles Lindbergh was kidnapped and murdered.

_____ **c.** In the 1930s different groups of Americans worked together for social justice.

_____ **d.** The Communist party had about 14,000 members.

____

GROUP 3

_____ **a.** Gangster Al Capone went to prison for tax evasion.

_____ **b.** Henry Ford, once admired for his efficiency, became labor's prime enemy.

_____ **c.** Symbols of the 1920s faded away.

_____ **d.** Depression humor was a successful weapon against widespread despair.

____

B. REVIEWING KEY TERMS

Answer the following question.

4. Why did most people support the *Twenty-first Amendment?* _______________________

____

GUIDED READING AND REVIEW   SECTION 4

The Election of 1932

A. AS YOU READ

As you read Section 4, fill in the missing information in the chart below.

HOOVER'S EFFORTS TO END THE DEPRESSION		
ACTION	GOAL	SUCCESS OR FAILURE/WHY?
organized White House conference of business leaders	1. to persuade business leaders voluntarily to maintain workers' wages	2.
signed the Hawley-Smoot tariff bill	3.	4.
set up Reconstruction Finance Corporation	5.	6.
insisted that state and local governments handle relief programs	7.	8.

B. REVIEWING KEY TERMS

Define or identify each of the following terms.

9. Hawley-Smoot tariff ____

10. Bonus Army ____

SECTION 1 | **GUIDED READING AND REVIEW**

Forging a New Deal

A. AS YOU READ

As you read Section 1, answer the following questions on the lines provided.

1. What steps did President Roosevelt take during his first few months in office

to reverse the trend of the Depression? _________________________________

____

2. How successful was the National Recovery Administration?

____

____

3. Who were FDR's advisers, and what did they do?

____

____

4. What caused the New Deal to falter?

____

____

5. What were some important characteristics of the Second New Deal programs?

____

____

6. What did FDR's landslide victory in the 1936 presidential election reveal about

Americans' response to the New Deal? _________________________________

____

B. REVIEWING KEY TERMS

Define or identify the following terms.

7. New Deal ____

8. hundred days ____

9. public works programs ____

10. Tennessee Valley Authority (TVA) ___________________________________

11. Second New Deal ____

12. Wagner Act ____

13. Social Security system ____

GUIDED READING AND REVIEW   SECTION 2

The New Deal's Critics

A. AS YOU READ

As you read Section 2, fill in three details that support each of the following main ideas.

Main Idea: Although the New Deal helped many people during the Depression, some groups of Americans benefited little, if at all.

1. ____

2. ____

3. ____

Main Idea: Americans criticized Roosevelt's New Deal both for doing too much and for not doing enough.

4. ____

5. ____

6. ____

Main Idea: Roosevelt tried to "pack" the Supreme Court with justices who favored the New Deal, but he was unsuccessful.

7. ____

8. ____

9. ____

B. REVIEWING KEY TERMS

Explain how each of the following terms is related to criticism of the New Deal.

10. American Liberty League ____

____

11. demagogue ____

____

12. nationalization ____

____

SECTION 3 | **GUIDED READING AND REVIEW**

Last Days of the New Deal

A. AS YOU READ

As you read Section 3, write two sentences to support each of the following main ideas.

1. The New Deal did not "cure" the Depression.

____

____

2. The New Deal had a significant impact on labor unions.

____

____

3. Radio and movies became popular forms of family entertainment during the 1930s.

____

____

4. Government projects helped to support writers, artists, musicians, and others during the Depression.

____

____

5. The New Deal had many lasting effects.

____

____

B. REVIEWING KEY TERMS

Define or identify each of the following terms.

6. national debt____

7. revenue ____

8. coalition ____

9. sit-down strike____

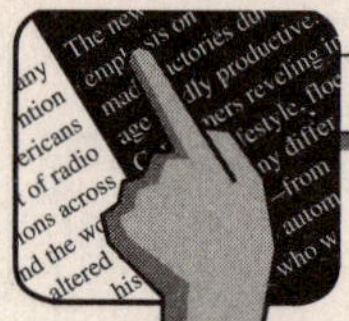

GUIDED READING AND REVIEW | SECTION 1

The Rise of Dictators

A. AS YOU READ

Below are four main ideas from Section 1. As you read, fill in at least two supporting facts under each main idea.

Main Idea: As a result of Stalin's plans to modernize agriculture and pursue industrialization, many people of the Soviet Union experienced severe living conditions.

1. ____

2. ____

Main Idea: Mussolini and the Fascists used aggressive tactics both within and outside of Italy.

3. ____

4. ____

Main Idea: The Great Depression severely affected Germany and contributed to the rise of Hitler and the Nazis.

5. ____

6. ____

Main Idea: Hitler pursued a policy of military and territorial expansion.

7. ____

8. ____

B. REVIEWING KEY TERMS

Define or identify each of the following terms.

9. totalitarian ____

10. fascism ____

11. Axis Powers ____

12. appeasement ____

SECTION 2 | **GUIDED READING AND REVIEW**

Europe Goes to War

A. As You Read

As you read Section 2, answer the following questions on the lines provided.

1. Why did Britain and France abandon their policy of appeasement?

____

____

2. What benefit did Hitler gain by signing a pact with Stalin?

____

____

3. How did Hitler's invasion of Poland expand the war?

____

____

4. What were the limitations of the Maginot Line?

____

____

5. Why were the events at Dunkirk memorable in military history?

____

____

6. What was the difference between Vichy France and Free France?

____

____

B. Reviewing Key Terms

Define or identify the following terms.

7. *blitzkrieg*

____

8. Resistance

____

9. Allies

____

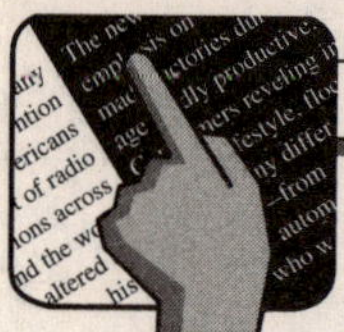

GUIDED READING AND REVIEW   **SECTION 3**

Japan Builds an Empire

A. AS YOU READ

As you read Section 3, draw a line through the term or name in each group that is not related to the others. Explain how the remaining terms or names are related.

1. high tariffs   Allies   Depression   political discontent

____

____

2. Germany   population growth   Manchuria   undeveloped land

____

____

3. Manchukuo   Manchurian Incident   puppet state   multi-party government

____

____

4. Jiang Jieshi   Europe   Mao Zedong   Japan-China war

____

____

5. Japan   Dutch East Indies   Burma Road   co-prosperity sphere

____

____

B. REVIEWING KEY TERMS

Complete the sentences below.

6. A *puppet state* is a supposedly independent country under the control of _______________

____

7. The *Burma Road* allowed Britain to send supplies to _______________________________

____

8. The real reason that Japan announced the *Greater East Asia Co-Prosperity Sphere* was that

____

____

SECTION 4 | **GUIDED READING AND REVIEW**

From Isolationism to War

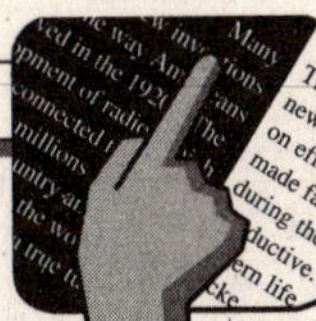

A. AS YOU READ

As you read Section 4, complete the sequence chain below to describe events relating to America's gradual change from isolationism to war.

1. In the early 1930s the government was more concerned with solving Depression-related problems than with international affairs.

2.

3.

4.

5.

6.

7.

8.

9.

B. REVIEWING KEY TERMS

Define the following terms and tell how each relates to isolationism.

10. Neutrality Acts

____

____

11. cash and carry

____

____

12. America First Committee

____

____

13. Lend-Lease Act

____

____

GUIDED READING AND REVIEW   SECTION 1

Mobilization

A. AS YOU READ

As you read Section 1, explain the role each of the following played in the shift from a peacetime to a wartime economy.

1. War Production Board ____

____

2. James F. Byrnes ____

____

3. Ford Motor Company ____

____

4. Henry J. Kaiser ____

____

5. "cost-plus" system ____

____

6. John L. Lewis ____

____

7. bond drives ____

____

B. REVIEWING KEY TERMS

Define or identify each of the following terms.

8. Selective Training and Service Act ______________________________________

____

9. Office of War Mobilization ____

____

10. Liberty ship ____

____

11. victory garden ____

____

SECTION 2 | **GUIDED READING AND REVIEW**

Retaking Europe

A. AS YOU READ

As you read Section 2, fill in the boxes below with details about the military campaigns in Europe during World War II.

Early Axis Dominance (1940–1942)

1. in the Atlantic:

2. in North Africa:

3. in the Soviet Union:

↓

Turnaround: Allied Offensives (1942–1944)

4. in North Africa:

5. in Italy:

↓

Victory in Europe (1944–1945)

6. in France:

7. in Germany:

B. REVIEWING KEY TERMS

Define or identify each of the following terms.

8. Atlantic Charter ____

9. carpet bombing ____

10. D-Day ____

11. Battle of the Bulge ____

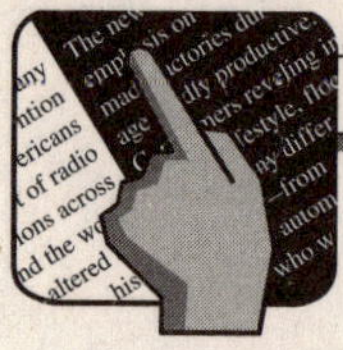

GUIDED READING AND REVIEW   SECTION 3

The Holocaust

A. AS YOU READ

As you read Section 3, explain the role that each of the following played during the Holocaust.

1. Nuremberg Laws

____

____

2. *Kristallnacht*

____

____

3. Evian Conference

____

____

4. Wannsee Conference

____

____

5. death camps

____

____

6. Nuremberg Trials

____

____

B. REVIEWING KEY TERMS

Answer the following questions.

7. What was the *Holocaust*? _______________________________

____

8. How did *anti-Semitism* affect Jews in Germany during the war? ___________

____

9. What was a *death camp*? How did it differ from a *concentration camp*? ___________

____

10. What was the purpose of the *War Refugee Board*? ___________

____

SECTION 4 | **GUIDED READING AND REVIEW**

The War in the Pacific

A. AS YOU READ

As you read Section 4, answer the following questions on the lines provided.

1. What actions did the Japanese take in the months after bombing Pearl Harbor?

____

____

2. How did the Allies stop the Japanese from overrunning Australia?

____

____

3. How did the Allies turn the tide of the war in the Pacific?

____

____

4. What success did the Allies have with their island-hopping strategy?

____

____

5. How did the decision to build and use atomic bombs on Japan come about?

____

____

6. What effects did the dropping of atomic bombs have?

____

____

B. REVIEWING KEY TERMS

Explain the impact of each term or pair of terms on the war in the Pacific.

7. Bataan Death March ____

8. Battle of the Coral Sea ____

9. Battle of Midway, Battle of Guadalcanal _______________________________

10. *kamikaze* ____

11. Battle of Iwo Jima, Battle of Okinawa ________________________________

12. Manhattan Project ____

GUIDED READING AND REVIEW SECTION 5

The Social Impact of the War

A. As You Read

As you read Section 5, write two sentences on the lines provided to support each of the following main ideas.

Main Idea: Although African Americans made some gains during the war years, they continued to suffer discrimination.

1. ____

2. ____

Main Idea: Mexican Americans found new employment opportunities during the war, but they also encountered discrimination.

3. ____

4. ____

Main Idea: Japanese Americans suffered discrimination and hostility during the war.

5. ____

6. ____

Main Idea: The war created new employment opportunities for women.

7. ____

8. ____

B. Reviewing Key Terms

Define the following terms.

9. Congress of Racial Equality (CORE) _______________________________

____

10. *bracero* ____

____

SECTION 1 | **GUIDED READING AND REVIEW**

Origins of the Cold War

A. As You Read

Below are three main ideas from Section 1. As you read, fill in two supporting facts under each main idea.

Main Idea: Relations between the United States and the Soviet Union were strained during the war and became even more tense as time passed.

1. ____

2. ____

Main Idea: The Soviet Union took control of the nations of Eastern Europe.

3. ____

4. ____

Main Idea: After the war, Americans disagreed about which political approach to take toward Soviet-American relations.

5. ____

6. ____

B. Reviewing Key Terms

Define or identify each of the following terms.

7. satellite nation ____

8. iron curtain ____

9. Cold War ____

10. Truman Doctrine ____

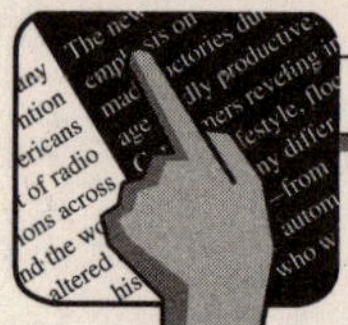

GUIDED READING AND REVIEW   **SECTION 2**

The Cold War Heats Up

A. AS YOU READ
As you read Section 2, complete the following sentences.

1. Through the Marshall Plan, the United States hoped to ___________________

____

2. By ordering the Berlin airlift, President Truman succeeded in ______________

____

3. The formation of NATO was proposed in order to _______________________

____

4. Two events that occurred in 1949 that increased American concerns about the
Cold War were ____

____

5. Loyalty programs proved unfair because _______________________________

____

B. REVIEWING KEY TERMS
Define or identify each of the following terms.

6. collective security ____

7. Warsaw Pact ____

8. House Un-American Activities Committee ______________________________

9. Hollywood Ten ____

10. blacklist ____

11. McCarren-Walter Act ____

SECTION 3 | **GUIDED READING AND REVIEW**

The Korean War

A. AS YOU READ
As you read Section 3, answer the following questions on the lines provided.

1. What events led to the "temporary" division of Korea? _________________________

____

2. How did the Korean War begin? _______________________________________

____

3. Why was the Korean War often referred to as a "UN police action" rather than a war? ________

____

4. How did General MacArthur contribute to UN success in the Korean War?

____

____

5. Why was the American public frustrated with the outcome of the Korean War?

____

____

6. What effect did the Korean War have on the federal budget?

____

____

B. REVIEWING KEY TERMS
Define or identify each of the following terms.

7. 38th parallel ____

8. Korean War ____

9. military-industrial complex ____

GUIDED READING AND REVIEW　　SECTION 4

The Continuing Cold War

A. As You Read

As you read Section 4, write one or two sentences to support each of the following main ideas.

Main Idea: Senator Joseph McCarthy's smear tactics spread suspicion and fear.

1. ____

____

Main Idea: President Eisenhower felt that the United States should not become involved in the affairs of Soviet Union satellite countries in Eastern Europe.

2. ____

____

Main Idea: The Cold War was waged on several fronts in the Middle East.

3. ____

____

Main Idea: During the 1950s the United States and the Soviet Union engaged in an arms race.

4. ____

____

Main Idea: U.S. anxiety increased as Americans witnessed advances in Soviet technology.

5. ____

____

B. Reviewing Key Terms

Define or identify the following terms.

6. arms race ___________________________________

____

7. deterrence __________________________________

____

8. brinkmanship ________________________________

____

9. *Sputnik* ___________________________________

____

10. U-2 incident ________________________________

____

SECTION 1 | **GUIDED READING AND REVIEW**

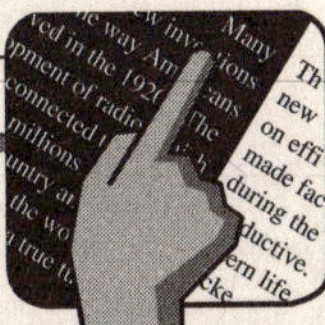

The Postwar Economy

A. AS YOU READ
As you read Section 1, answer the following questions.

BUSINESS EXPANSION

1. In the 1950s, how did some corporations expand to protect themselves against the dangers of economic downturns?

2. What were the main advantages of the franchise system?

NEW TECHNOLOGY

3. How did television contribute to the growth of consumer spending?

4. Why was the invention of the transistor significant?

5. How did research for the atomic bomb lead to a new industry?

CHANGING LIVES

6. What were the advantages and drawbacks of white-collar work?

7. What made the suburbs expand?

8. How did suburban expansion lead to the growth of the auto industry, highways, and consumer credit?

B. REVIEWING KEY TERMS
Use each of the following terms in a sentence that shows the meaning of the term.

9. per capita income _______________________________________

10. conglomerate _______________________________________

11. transistor _______________________________________

12. baby boom _______________________________________

13. GI Bill of Rights _______________________________________

GUIDED READING AND REVIEW   SECTION 2

The Mood of the 1950s

A. AS YOU READ

Complete each sentence below as you read Section 2.

1. Young people of the 1950s were sometimes known as the "silent generation" *because*

____

____

2. During the 1950s teenagers were more likely to remain in school than to go to work *because*

____

____

3. A religious resurgence occurred in the 1950s *because* _______________________________

____

____

4. Some women chose not to give up their jobs *because* _______________________________

____

____

5. In her book *The Feminine Mystique*, Betty Friedan charged that many women were frustrated
because ____

____

6. Young people of the 1950s challenged the norms of society *because* _______________________

____

____

7. Many adults disliked rock-and-roll music *because* _______________________________

____

____

B. REVIEWING KEY TERMS

Define or identify each of the following terms.

8. rock-and-roll ____

9. beatnik ____

SECTION 3 | **GUIDED READING AND REVIEW**

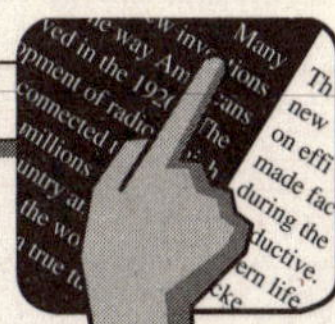

Domestic Politics and Policy

A. AS YOU READ

As you read Section 3, write one or two supporting details under each of the following main ideas.

1. President Truman had difficulty helping the economy make the transition from wartime to peacetime.

____

____

2. Truman's Fair Deal met with fierce opposition in Congress.

____

____

3. Truman's reelection in 1948 was an upset.

____

____

4. Eisenhower won the presidency in 1952 despite his running mate's difficulties.

____

____

5. Eisenhower supported the interests of big business.

____

____

6. The launch of *Sputnik* challenged Americans' sense of security and self-confidence.

____

____

B. REVIEWING KEY TERMS

Define or identify each of the following terms.

7. Taft-Hartley Act ____

8. modern republicanism ____

9. National Defense Education Act _________________________________

GUIDED READING AND REVIEW   SECTION 1

Demands for Civil Rights

A. As You Read

As you read Section 1, check the sentence in each group that is not related to the other sentences. Then write another related sentence on the line provided.

Group 1

______   **a.** The number of African Americans employed by the federal government increased greatly under Roosevelt.

______   **b.** Prominent African American citizens emerged from the expanding urban black population.

______   **c.** Thurgood Marshall joined the NAACP in the 1930s.

______   **d.** African Americans gained voting power in some northern cities.

____

Group 2

______   **a.** Mexican Americans found that peaceful protest could bring change.

______   **b.** Thurgood Marshall argued against the "separate but equal" doctrine.

______   **c.** Martin Luther King, Jr., became the spokesperson for the protest movement in Montgomery, Alabama.

______   **d.** In 1955, Rosa Parks refused to give up her seat on a bus.

____

Group 3

______   **a.** Southern whites confronted black students attempting to enter Central High School in Little Rock.

______   **b.** The federal government adopted a policy known as "termination."

______   **c.** Eisenhower took control of the Arkansas National Guard.

______   **d.** Governor Orville Faubus refused to enforce integration.

____

B. Reviewing Key Terms

Explain how each of the following related to the struggle for equality. Write your answers on the back of this sheet of paper or on a separate sheet.

4. *Brown* v. *Board of Education of Topeka, Kansas*

5. Montgomery bus boycott

6. integration

SECTION 2 | **GUIDED READING AND REVIEW**

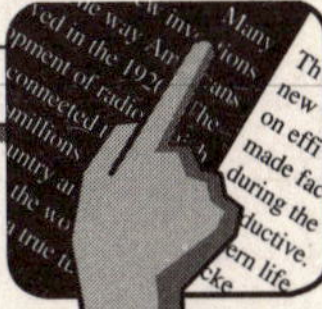

Leaders and Strategies

A. As You Read

As you read Section 2, write two sentences for each of the following civil rights groups that describe the role that group played in the civil rights movement.

National Association for the Advancement of Colored People (NAACP)

1. ____
2. ____

National Urban League

3. ____
4. ____

Congress of Racial Equality (CORE)

5. ____
6. ____

Southern Christian Leadership Conference (SCLC)

7. ____
8. ____

Student Nonviolent Coordinating Committee (SNCC)

9. ____
10. ____

B. Reviewing Key Terms

Use each of the following terms in a sentence that reveals the term's meaning.

11. interracial ____

____

12. nonviolent protest ____

____

GUIDED READING AND REVIEW | SECTION 3

The Struggle Intensifies

A. AS YOU READ

As you read Section 3, check the sentence in each group that is not related to the other sentences. Then write another related sentence on the line provided.

GROUP 1

_______ **a.** Sit-ins were one of the most successful tools of the civil rights movement.

_______ **b.** Sit-ins gained the support of the SCLC.

_______ **c.** The goal of the sit-in was to disrupt business at a lunch counter or other public place until it abolished its segregation policies.

_______ **d.** In a 1960 ruling the Supreme Court expanded the ban on segregation of buses.

____

GROUP 2

_______ **a.** James Meredith was denied admission to the University of Mississippi on racial grounds.

_______ **b.** CORE led an effort to test the Supreme Court decision in *Boynton* v. *Virginia*.

_______ **c.** Robert Kennedy assigned federal marshals to protect the Freedom Riders.

_______ **d.** Policemen in Anniston, Alabama, did not try to stop a white mob who firebombed a bus full of civil rights activists.

____

GROUP 3

_______ **a.** Televised scenes of police violence in Birmingham appalled Americans.

_______ **b.** The protest became a standoff between Mississippi and the Justice Department.

_______ **c.** Police used high-pressure fire hoses on the demonstrators.

_______ **d.** Trained police dogs attacked the civil rights marchers.

____

B. REVIEWING KEY TERMS

Define or identify each of the following terms.

4. sit-in ____

5. Freedom Ride ____

© Pearson Education, Inc.

SECTION 4 | **GUIDED READING AND REVIEW**

The Political Response

A. AS YOU READ

As you read Section 4, fill in three supporting facts under each main idea statement.

Main Idea: President Kennedy took steps to promote civil rights and eliminate racial discrimination.

1. ____

2. ____

3. ____

Main Idea: A historic protest march and pressure from President Johnson led to the passage of the Civil Rights Act of 1964.

4. ____

5. ____

6. ____

Main Idea: Continuing protests by African Americans led to further protection of their voting rights.

7. ____

8. ____

9. ____

B. REVIEWING KEY TERMS

Explain the significance of each of the following to the civil rights movement.

10. March on Washington ____

____

11. cloture ____

____

12. Civil Rights Act of 1964 ____

____

13. Voting Rights Act of 1965 ____

____

The Movement Takes a New Turn

A. AS YOU READ

As you read Section 5, answer the following questions on the lines provided.

1. According to James Baldwin, what impact had generations of oppression and suffering had on African Americans?

____

____

2. In what ways did Malcolm X disagree with the strategies and goals of the early civil rights leaders?

____

____

3. How did Stokely Carmichael change SNCC?

____

____

4. What conditions in the late 1960s led to widespread rioting in the nation's cities?

____

____

5. What were some important social and political changes brought about by the civil rights movement?

____

____

B. REVIEWING KEY TERMS

Define or identify each of the following terms.

6. Nation of Islam ____

7. black nationalism ____

8. black power ____

9. *de jure* segregation ____

10. *de facto* segregation ____

SECTION 1 | **GUIDED READING AND REVIEW**

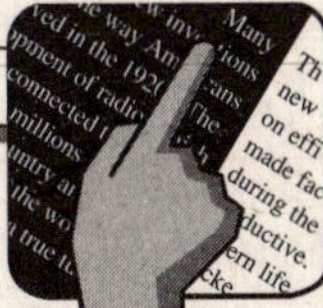

The New Frontier

A. As You Read

As you read Section 1, rewrite each sentence below to make it correct.

1. Richard Nixon's performance during the first televised presidential debate in 1960 impressed most viewers.

____

____

2. Democrat John F. Kennedy won the election of 1960 in a landslide.

____

____

3. The New Frontier favored the wishes of big business rather than the needs of the poor and minorities.

____

____

4. Most of President Kennedy's bold initiatives became law.

____

____

5. Kennedy refused to support the U.S. space program.

____

____

6. The Warren Commission declared that the Kennedy assassination was part of a larger conspiracy.

____

____

B. Reviewing Key Terms

Answer each of the following questions.

7. Why did Kennedy lack a *mandate* to push his measures through Congress?

____

8. What were the key elements of the *New Frontier*?

____

9. Why was the *Warren Commission* needed?

____

GUIDED READING AND REVIEW **SECTION 2**

The Great Society

A. AS YOU READ

As you read Section 2, fill in the missing information in the chart below.

THE GREAT SOCIETY	
Program or Legislation	**Description**
1.	revived prosperity and decreased unemployment
Economic Opportunity Act	2.
Elementary and Secondary Education Act	3.
4.	provided hospital care and low-cost medical insurance for Americans age 65 and older
Medicaid	5.
6.	replaced quotas with more flexible limits
Criticisms	
7.	
8.	
9.	

B. REVIEWING KEY TERMS

Define or identify each of the following terms.

10. Great Society ____

11. Volunteers in Service to America (VISTA) ___________________________

12. Miranda rule ____

13. apportionment ____

SECTION 3 | **GUIDED READING AND REVIEW**

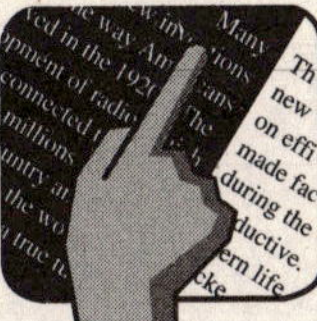

Foreign Policy in the Early 1960s

A. As You Read

As you read Section 3, fill in the missing information in the chart below.

FOREIGN POLICY IN THE EARLY 1960s		
ACTION	**GOAL**	**RESULT**
Kennedy supported an invasion of the Bay of Pigs	1. to encourage the Cuban people to overthrow Fidel Castro	2.
Kennedy met with Soviet leader Nikita Khrushchev in June 1961	3.	4.
Kennedy authorized a naval quarantine around Cuba	5.	6.
Kennedy established the Alliance for Progress	7.	8.
Johnson sent 22,000 marines to the Dominican Republic	9.	10.

B. Reviewing Key Terms

Identify each of the following terms.

11. Berlin Wall ____

12. Cuban Missile Crisis ____

13. Limited Test Ban Treaty ____

14. Peace Corps ____

GUIDED READING AND REVIEW | SECTION 1

The Women's Movement

A. AS YOU READ

As you read Section 1, answer the following questions on the lines provided.

1. What conditions in society helped bring about the women's movement in the 1960s?

____

____

2. What experiences did women gain while working in the civil rights movement that helped them later in the women's movement?

____

____

3. What factors helped raise women's consciousness of social issues related to women?

____

____

4. Why was the National Organization for Women (NOW) founded?

____

____

5. What differences divided the women's movement?

____

____

6. Who opposed the women's movement, and for what reasons?

____

____

B. REVIEWING KEY TERMS

Define or identify each of the following terms.

7. feminism ____

8. National Organization for Women (NOW) _______________________________

9. *Roe* v. *Wade* ____

10. Equal Rights Amendment (ERA) _______________________________________

© Pearson Education, Inc.

SECTION 2 | **GUIDED READING AND REVIEW**

Ethnic Minorities Seek Equality

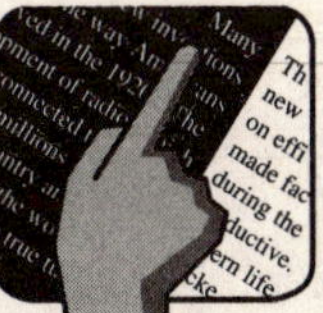

A. As You Read

Below are four main ideas from Section 2. As you read, fill in at least two supporting details under each main idea.

Main Idea: Latinos faced various forms of discrimination.

1. ____

2. ____

Main Idea: Latino activists brought about significant progress in labor and politics.

3. ____

4. ____

Main Idea: Asian Americans made some progress in their fight against discrimination.

5. ____

6. ____

Main Idea: Native Americans faced unique problems, which they tried to fight against, but achieved only limited success.

7. ____

8. ____

B. Reviewing Key Terms

Define or identify each of the following terms.

9. Latino ____

10. migrant farm worker ____

11. United Farm Workers (UFW) ____

12. American Indian Movement (AIM) ____

GUIDED READING AND REVIEW   SECTION 3

The Counterculture

A. As You Read

As you read Section 3, fill in the chart with details describing the counterculture.

ASPECTS OF THE COUNTERCULTURE	
1. Style and Fashion	**2.** Sexual Behavior
3. Drugs	**4.** Music

B. Reviewing Key Terms

Answer the following questions.

5. What were some characteristics of the *counterculture*?

____

____

6. What was the importance of the *Woodstock festival*?

____

____

SECTION 4 | **GUIDED READING AND REVIEW**

The Environmental and Consumer Movements

A. AS YOU READ

As you read Section 4, draw a line through the term or name in each group that is not related to the others. Explain how the remaining terms or names are related.

1. Rachel Carson   New Deal   DDT   *Silent Spring*

____

____

2. Sierra Club   Barry Commoner   bald eagles   Gaylord Nelson

____

____

3. Nuclear Regulatory Commission   Clean Air Act   Clean Water Act   Environmental Protection Agency

____

____

4. Ralph Nader   Alaska   automobiles   consumer movement

____

____

5. *Silent Spring*   *Washington Post*   *The Closing Circle*   *Unsafe at Any Speed*

____

____

B. REVIEWING KEY TERMS

Identify each of the following terms and explain its role in helping the environment.

6. Nuclear Regulatory Commission (NRC) _______________________________

____

7. Environmental Protection Agency (EPA) _______________________________

____

8. Clean Air Act ____

____

9. Clean Water Act ____

____

GUIDED READING AND REVIEW   SECTION 1

The War Unfolds

A. AS YOU READ

As you read Section 1, complete the chart by writing one effect of each cause.

1. Cause: The Geneva Accords are signed.	**1. Effect:** ___________________________
2. Cause: In 1960 President Eisenhower sends military advisers to help South Vietnam against North Vietnam.	**2. Effect:** ___________________________
3. Cause: Diem tells Vice President Johnson that South Vietnam needs more aid to survive.	**3. Effect:** ___________________________
4. Cause: United States officials suggested that they would not object to Diem's overthrow.	**4. Effect:** ___________________________
5. Cause: North Vietnamese torpedo boats attacked American destroyers in the Gulf of Tonkin.	**5. Effect:** ___________________________

B. REVIEWING KEY TERMS

Define or identify each of the following terms.

6. domino theory ____

7. Geneva Accords ____

8. Viet Cong ____

9. National Liberation Front ____

10. Gulf of Tonkin Resolution ____

SECTION 2   **GUIDED READING AND REVIEW**

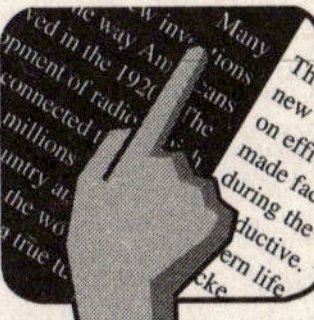

Fighting the War

A. As You Read

As you read Section 2, complete the outline. Write details about the realities of the war for American soldiers and for Vietnamese civilians.

I. AMERICAN SOLDIERS

A. What they encountered when they first arrived in Vietnam

   1.

   2.

B. What they experienced on the battlefield

   3.

   4.

   5.

II. VIETNAMESE CIVILIANS

A. What happened to the people

   6.

   7.

B. What happened to the land

   8.

   9.

B. Reviewing Key Terms

Define or identify each of the following terms.

10. land mine ____

11. saturation bombing ____

12. napalm ____

13. escalation ____

GUIDED READING AND REVIEW   SECTION 3

Political Divisions

A. AS YOU READ

As you read Section 3, write three supporting details under each of the following main ideas.

Main Idea: The 1960s were a time of student activism.

1. ____

2. ____

3. ____

Main Idea: The draft became a controversial issue during the Vietnam War.

4. ____

5. ____

6. ____

Main Idea: The Vietnam War significantly affected the election of 1968.

7. ____

8. ____

9. ____

B. REVIEWING KEY TERMS

Define or identify each of the following terms.

10. New Left ____

11. teach-in ____

12. conscientious objector ____

13. deferment ____

SECTION 4 | **GUIDED READING AND REVIEW**

The End of the War

A. As You Read

As you read Section 4, complete the sentences below.

1. During the presidential campaign, Richard Nixon claimed that ___________________________

____

2. The basic idea behind the policy of Vietmanization was ___________________________

____

3. Nixon withdrew troops from Vietnam and ordered bombing raids at the same

time because ____

____

4. Nixon widened the war by sending ground forces into Cambodia because ___________

____

5. Nixon's invasion of Cambodia led to ____

____

6. After the United States withdrew from Vietnam, South Vietnam _________________

____

7. The legacy of the Vietnam War included _______________________________________

____

B. Reviewing Key Terms

Complete the sentences below.

8. The *Paris peace talks* involved negotiations between ___________________________

____

9. According to Nixon, the *silent majority* included _____________________________

____

10. *POWs* and *MIAs* referred to ____

____

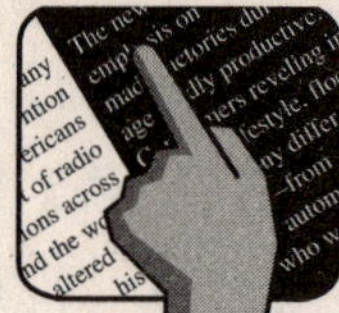

GUIDED READING AND REVIEW | SECTION 1

Nixon's Domestic Policy

A. AS YOU READ

As you read Section 1, write one or two sentences to support each of the following main ideas.

1. Nixon relied on handpicked "team players" to develop his policies and advise him.

____

____

2. Nixon was frustrated in his attempts to deal with inflation, unemployment, and the energy problem.

____

____

3. Developments in the Middle East caused problems in the United States.

____

____

4. Nixon's "southern strategy" slowed the advance of civil rights.

____

____

5. Nixon's views were apparent in the way he tried to reshape the Supreme Court.

____

____

B. REVIEWING KEY TERMS

Briefly define each of the following terms.

6. deficit spending ____

7. Organization of Petroleum Exporting Countries (OPEC) _______________

____

8. embargo ____

9. New Federalism ____

SECTION 2 **GUIDED READING AND REVIEW**

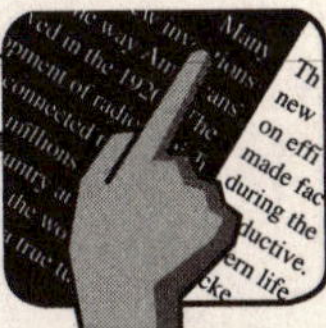

Nixon's Foreign Policy

A. As You Read

As you read Section 2, answer the following questions on the lines provided.

1. What role did Henry Kissinger play in shaping President Nixon's foreign policy?

____

____

2. How did Nixon's foreign policy affect relations between the United States and major Communist nations?

____

____

3. Why did Nixon decide to travel to China?

____

____

4. What types of agreements did Nixon make with Soviet premier Leonid Brezhnev?

____

____

5. How did a shift in Nixon's thinking about nuclear weapons pave the way for SALT I?

____

____

B. Reviewing Key Terms

Briefly explain the importance of each of the following in Nixon's foreign policy.

6. *realpolitik* ____

____

7. détente ____

____

8. SALT I ____

____

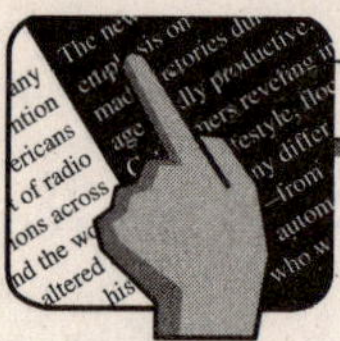

GUIDED READING AND REVIEW   SECTION 3

The Watergate Scandal

A. AS YOU READ

As you read Section 3, fill in the boxes in the sequence chain below to show how the Watergate scandal unfolded, ending with Nixon's resignation.

1. With Nixon's approval, a special White House unit is organized, which breaks into the office of Daniel Ellsberg's psychiatrist.

2.

3.

4.

5.

6.

7.

8.

9.

B. REVIEWING KEY TERMS

Explain the significance of each of the following terms to Nixon's presidency.

10. Watergate scandal ____

11. special prosecutor ____

12. impeach ____

SECTION 4 | **GUIDED READING AND REVIEW**

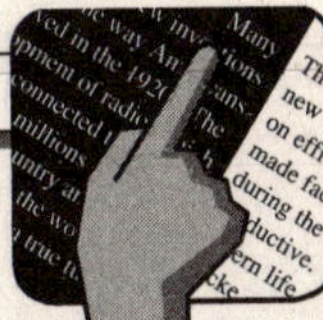

The Ford Administration

A. AS YOU READ

As you read Section 4, fill in three supporting details under each of the following main ideas from the section.

Main Idea: The positive mood of the public when Ford took office was dampened by his pardon of Nixon.

1. ____

2. ____

3. ____

Main Idea: President Ford had little success in dealing with the stalled economy or with the Democratic-controlled Congress.

4. ____

5. ____

6. ____

Main Idea: As President, Ford achieved several successes in foreign policy.

7. ____

8. ____

9. ____

B. REVIEWING KEY TERMS

Define or identify each of the following terms.

10. stagflation ____

11. War Powers Act ____

12. Helsinki Accords ____

13. bicentennial ____

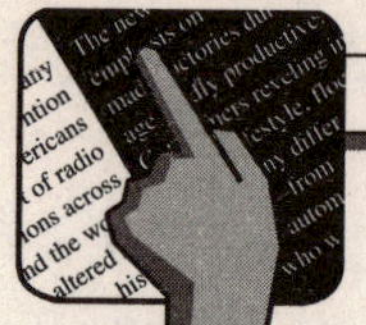

GUIDED READING AND REVIEW   SECTION 5

The Carter Administration

A. As You Read

As you read Section 5, answer the following questions on the lines provided.

1. In what ways was Carter's approach to the presidency different from that of his predecessors? ____

____

2. Why did the nation lose confidence in Carter's ability to help the economy?

____

____

3. What efforts did Carter make to deal with the problem of rising oil prices?

____

____

4. What was the significance of Allan Bakke's Supreme Court case?

____

____

5. What compromise formed the basis of the Camp David Accords?

____

____

6. What caused the Iran hostage crisis? ___________________________________

____

B. Reviewing Key Terms

Define the following terms.

7. incumbent ____

8. deregulation ____

9. amnesty ____

10. affirmative action ____

11. dissident ____

NAME ______________________ CLASS ______________ DATE ______________

SECTION 1 **GUIDED READING AND REVIEW**

Roots of the New Conservatism

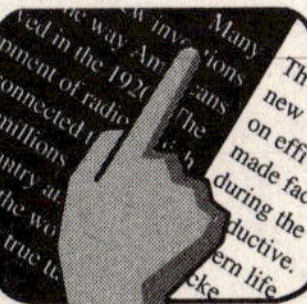

A. As You Read

As you read Section 1, fill in the graphic organizer. Explain the relationship of each person to the conservative movement.

The Conservative Movement

1. Franklin D. Roosevelt
2. Barry Goldwater
3. Lyndon Johnson
4. Richard Nixon
5. Jerry Falwell
6. Ronald Reagan

B. Reviewing Key Terms

Explain how each of the following relates to the conservative movement.

7. New Right ______________________________

8. televangelism ______________________________

GUIDED READING AND REVIEW   SECTION 2

The Reagan Revolution

A. AS YOU READ

As you read Section 2, write in each of the missing causes and effects.

1. Cause: Reagan pushed tax cuts and tax reform through Congress.	**1. Effect:** _________________________ _________________________
2. Cause: _________________________ _________________________	**2. Effect:** States did not have enough money for programs formerly funded by the federal government.
3. Cause: Reagan greatly expanded spending on defense to counter the Soviet threat.	**3. Effect:** _________________________ _________________________
4. Cause: Reagan sought ways to protect Americans from nuclear attack.	**4. Effect:** _________________________ _________________________
5. Cause: _________________________ _________________________	**5. Effect:** American troops were pulled out of Lebanon.

Write your own cause-and-effect statements about the Reagan revolution.

6. Cause: _________________________ _________________________	**6. Effect:** _________________________ _________________________

B. REVIEWING KEY TERMS

Explain how each of the following relates to the Reagan revolution.

7. supply-side economics ____

8. New Federalism ____

9. Strategic Defense Initiative (SDI) ____

SECTION 3 | **GUIDED READING AND REVIEW**

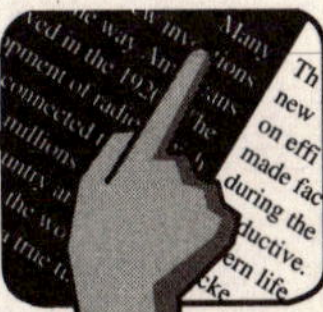

Reagan's Second Term

A. AS YOU READ

As you read Section 3, complete the chart below by describing events and issues
of President Reagan's second term.

ISSUE/EVENT	DESCRIPTION
1. Bicentennial of the Constitution	
2. Extension of the Voting Rights Act	
3. Supreme Court appointments	
4. S & L scandal	
5. Iran-Contra affair	
6. INF Treaty	
7. Growth of entitlement programs	

B. REVIEWING KEY TERMS

Explain the significance of each of the following during Reagan's second term.

8. AIDS ____

9. Sandinistas ____

10. Contras ____

11. entitlement ____

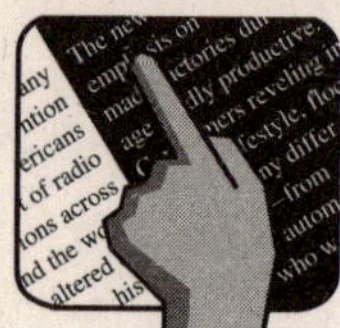

GUIDED READING AND REVIEW | **SECTION 4**

The George H. W. Bush Administration

A. As You Read

As you read Section 4, fill in three supporting details under each main idea.

Main Idea: George Bush's strategies proved effective in the 1988 presidential campaign.

1. ____

2. ____

3. ____

Main Idea: During George H. W. Bush's presidency, significant events occurred in many parts of the world.

4. ____

5. ____

6. ____

Main Idea: Domestic problems weakened Bush's popularity.

7. ____

8. ____

9. ____

B. Reviewing Key Terms

Explain the significance of each of the following to the Bush presidency.

10. Strategic Arms Reduction Treaty (START) ______________________________

____

11. Persian Gulf War ____

____

12. downsizing ____

____

SECTION 1 | **GUIDED READING AND REVIEW**

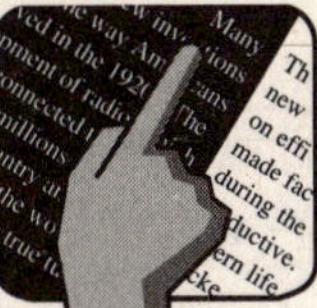

Politics in Recent Years

A. As You Read

As you read Section 1, answer the following questions on the lines provided.

1. How did the campaigns of the three candidates during the 1992 presidential election differ? ____

____

2. How successful was Clinton in dealing with problems in the healthcare system? ____

____

3. How did the clash between Clinton and Gingrich hurt the Republicans and help Clinton? ____

____

4. What factors contributed to Clinton's reelection in 1996? _______________________

____

5. What events tarnished Clinton's second term in office? _____________________

____

6. Why did Florida become a battleground in the 2000 presidential election? _____________

____

7. What destructive event shocked the nation less than nine months after George W. Bush took office? ____

____

B. Reviewing Key Terms

Describe the impact that each of the following had on Clinton's presidency.

8. Contract with America ____

____

9. Whitewater affair ____

____

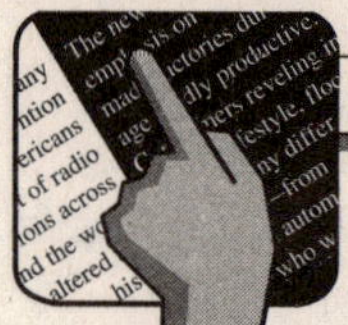

GUIDED READING AND REVIEW   SECTION 2

The United States in a New World

A. AS YOU READ

As you read Section 2, write two sentences on the lines provided to support each of the following main ideas.

Main Idea: Significant political changes occurred in Russia, Eastern Europe, and South Africa during the 1990s.

1. ____

2. ____

Main Idea: The quest for peace in the Middle East met with only limited success.

3. ____

4. ____

Main Idea: The United States and NATO worked to put an end to the violence in the Balkans.

5. ____

6. ____

Main Idea: The issue of Taiwan strained relations between the United States and China.

7. ____

8. ____

B. REVIEWING KEY TERMS

Answer each of the following questions on the back of this sheet of paper or on a separate sheet.

9. What is *apartheid*, and how did it affect South Africa?

10. Why did the United States and other nations impose *economic sanctions* on South Africa in the mid-1980s?

11. What is the purpose of the *North American Free Trade Agreement (NAFTA)*?

12. What is the purpose of the *World Trade Organization (WTO)*?

SECTION 3 | **GUIDED READING AND REVIEW**

Americans in the New Millennium

A. AS YOU READ
As you read Section 3, complete the outline by answering the questions below.

I. Immigration patterns changed near the end of the twentieth century.

1. Where did most immigrants come from in the 1990s?

____

2. How did the Immigration Act of 1965 help bring this about?

____

3. Where did many of the new immigrants settle?

____

4. What effect has the growing minority population had on politics?

____

II. Americans have struggled to make diversity work.

5. What aspects of this struggle have led to controversy, and why?

____

6. Why have some people called for a tougher immigration policy?

____

B. REVIEWING KEY TERMS
Complete the following sentences.

7. *Multiculturalism* was a movement that called for _______________________________________

____

8. The *Internet* is a computer network that _______________________________________

____